LEADERSHIP BURNOUT AND RECOVERY

Praise for Don Womble and
Leadership Burnout and Recovery

"In his new book, *Leadership Burnout and Recovery*, Don gives us a blueprint (from his own deep life experiences) of a more holistic and centered way to lead, as well as a path forward to recovery … from past mistakes, wounds, failures, and even heartbreak.

If you're on a leadership journey of any sort, Don's words will speak life and healing to you, especially to the places in your story that need it most."

—Brent McCorkle
Writer/Film Director—Jesus Revolution—I Can Only Imagine

"Don Womble has written a compelling description of his burnout experience and recovery that has led to the reaching of thousands through his post-burnout career…everyone should be aware of the signs of burnout in their lives and this book, and its practical nature and real-world solutions will help you learn from one who has been there and come out on the other side even stronger."

—Hon. Andrew L. Wambsganss
Brown Pruitt Wambsganss Dean Forman & Moore, PC

"This book hears and answers the cry of the burned-out soul. Expect to be challenged to the point of healing by someone who has been there and done that."

—Adam McCain
Provost, Christ for the Nations
Lead Pastor, Hill City Church

"As a leader for 25+ years, I can only wish I would have had Don Womble's book, *Leadership Burnout and Recovery* to read years ago. This book is a real eye opener for leaders, young and old… a must read! I highly recommend this book. We have always heard 'we are our own worst enemy.' This is especially true with leaders. I highly recommend you read Don Womble's book."

—Billy P. Davis,
Mayor, Crowley, Tx

"Don's 30/60/90-day plan for personal growth through your noted journal, a vision, and sharing it with others is the recovering road to putting burnout in the rear-view mirror. An exceptional book that brings recognition of a problem that plagues many in leadership while motivating us to return to the mindset that first encouraged us to be leaders."

—Jeff Gilbert
President/Sole Owner of Fun-n-Sun Sports Center Ltd.
Partner of Beaumont Express
Chicken Express Franchises

"In a world obsessed with "normal", Don Womble's book dares to whisper, "It's okay to admit that one needs help". At times it can be a quiet, dramatic break or even a soul-crushing kind that creeps in when the weight of societal expectations and personal pressures become too much to bear. Womble doesn't just acknowledge this invisible epidemic; he offers a hand up, a step-by-step guide to rising from the ashes of burnout.

Forget the stiff upper lip and toxic positivity. This book is a sanctuary for the weary and a roadmap for navigating the tangled jungle of stress. It confronts head-on the societal shame that silences struggle, then gently dismantles it brick by brick. Refreshingly, it not only diagnoses the present but inoculates the future, offering practical tools to prevent these debilitating crashes before they even start.

I urge you, whether you're drowning in burnout or merely treading water, to dive into this book. For within its pages lies a lifeline, a beacon of hope for not just the burned-out soul but for the compassionate friend, the supportive colleague and anyone who longs to help but doesn't know how. Together, let's rewrite the narrative where vulnerability isn't weakness but the first step towards strength."

—Bruce O'Neal
President Emeritus, MANNA Worldwide

"Discover a transformative journey through the pages of this book, where Don masterfully unveils timeless principles of leadership resilience. A compelling must-read for anyone navigating the daunting challenges of burnout, Don shares his own courageous odyssey from thriving leader to personal and professional crisis with unwavering transparency. Through his poignant narrative, he not only offers invaluable insights but also presents practical strategies for healing, including a user-friendly 90-day recovery plan. Whether you're seeking spiritual renewal or emotional fortitude, this book is a beacon of hope and restoration for leaders at every stage of their journey."

—Roger Saade, MD
TotalCare Clinic

"Don offers readers a personal and authentic view into his story of navigating the onset of burnout and into successful recovery. He provides both understanding and encouragement to anyone experiencing these challenges with practical application steps to embrace on their own road to recovery."

—Mike Wroughton
Chief Strategy Officer, Powerhouse Services

"*Leadership Burnout and Recovery* helped me to discover so many things about myself. Early on in Don's book, I thought I was going to jump out of my seat when he gave the analogy of the frog who essentially gets comfortable with the slow rising temperature water. I thought to myself how guilty I am of doing the same. I now realize that my work/life balance is necessary to show up for myself and others each day! Thank you, Don!"

—Trina Lane
Executive Director of Counseling Services, M.Ed, Crowley ISD, Texas

"Don Womble's *Leadership Burnout and Recovery* hits home in a way that many leadership books don't. I've been down the burnout road myself, and back then, I didn't have a guide like this.

Don doesn't beat around the bush. He spills it all—the struggles, the real deal behind burnout, and what it took for him to bounce back. Reading this book feels like having a heart-to-heart with a mentor who's been through the trenches and came out wiser.

What I appreciate most is the down-to-earth advice. It's not some high and mighty strategy that only works in an ideal world. Don shares real, actionable things—from dealing with the daily grind to finding your way back when you've hit rock bottom.

Leadership Burnout and Recovery isn't just another leadership book; it's a life preserver for anyone who's ever felt the weight of leadership on their shoulders and feels like they are going to go under. Don's been there, and he's got your back with practical wisdom and a roadmap for recovery.

If you're a leader—seasoned or just starting out—and you've ever felt that burnout grind, grab this book. It's like getting advice from a friend who's been in your shoes and knows the way out.

—Keith Leonhardt
Cleburne, Texas

"Don Womble's voice of experience speaks volumes to the suffers of this pit of despair. This book will guide you or anyone you know to the light at the end of the tunnel."

—Jim Dillow, Entrepreneur

"Don Womble is a man whose priorities are in order, and he knows what he is talking about from his considerable experience in ministry and leading people. This book is practical, passionate, and powerful! I know it will benefit anyone who takes the time to both read and apply the principles he talks about. It is a joy to recommend it to you."

—Bill Ramsey
Church Planter / Lead Pastor—The Met, Fort Worth, Texas

"This book is a great navigation guide to recognize if burnout is something you struggle with and how to work through that to become a better character, not just in the workplace but all around. I'm a teacher and burnout is something that many teachers face and is why we lose so many educators very early on in their careers. When reading through the burnout identifiers I was able to easily connect with many of them. Such as:
- Being overwhelmed
- Having feelings of failure/not being good enough
- Feeling drained easily
- Not being as joyful in the workplace

My big takeaway from this journey of recovery from burnout is having a healthy mindset. Being in a growth mindset is something that's instilled in us as teachers because this is a career that's constantly having to adapt. This book helped me identify key aspects to a healthy mindset and exercises I can do to help maintain this day to day. *Leadership Burnout and Recovery* is a book that can be used for people that see burnout peaking over the horizon or are already experiencing burnout. This book gives you exercises for each specific identifier of burnout and how you can work on becoming a better you."

—Kristian Nicole
Educator

LEADERSHIP BURNOUT AND RECOVERY

*From One Who Was
Burned Out and Broken*

DON WOMBLE

LEADERSHIP BURNOUT AND RECOVERY
From One Who Was Burned Out and Broken

Copyright ©2023 by Don Womble
All rights reserved.

No part of this publication may be reproduced, stored in a retrieval system, or transmitted in any form or by any means—electronic, mechanical, photocopy, recording, or any other—without the prior permission of the author.

Some names and characteristics have been changed, some events have been compressed, and some dialogue has been recreated.

ISBN Paperback: 978-1-7386416-9-7
ISBN eBook: 978-1-7380493-0-1

Published by: Helping People Press, a wholly owned subsidiary of The Authority Factory, Toronto, Canada

Dedication

I dedicate this book to Brent Teeter. He believed in me and gave me the opportunity to lead again upon my recovery from burnout.

TABLE OF CONTENTS

Foreword by Master Coach LaKendra Smalley ix

Introduction xi
   Why Should You Trust Me? xiii
   The Voyage xv

CHAPTER ONE: I Am Lost and Broken 1
   Realize It 3
   Admit It to Quit It 8
   Have No Fear 11
   Trade Your Pride for Humility 14
   EXERCISE: Finding and Fixing Me. 15

CHAPTER TWO: What Am I Supposed to Do? 17
   Discover Your True Self 17
   Build Self-Respect 19
   Life Goes On. 20
   Be Authentically You 27
   EXERCISE: Learn and Grow. 31

CHAPTER THREE: Painfully You—The Anchors 33
   Self-Imposed Troubles—You Did It 33
   Betrayal 35
   Isolation 37
   Lack of Self-Care. 38
   Entrapment 40
   Nasty Secret Addictions 42
   Infidelity. 43

    Fragmented Relationships 45
    In Summary 48
    EXERCISE: Out with the Old 51

CHAPTER FOUR: Forgive the Pain Away **53**
    Resentment 53
    Guilt 54
    Bitterness or Blame 55
    Forgiveness 56
    How Do I Forgive? 61
    EXERCISE: Forgive the Pain Away 67

CHAPTER FIVE: Recovering You—Healthy Habits **69**
    Don't Let Bad Habits Sink Your Ship 71
    Good Habits Keep Your Ship Afloat 74
    Positive and Healthy Habits for Smooth Sailing 74
    EXERCISE: In With the New 80

**CHAPTER SIX: Recovering You—Keeping Account
           of Your Ability** **81**
    Accountability Is Not that Difficult, Don't Make It Hard 85
    Family Time—Make it Educational and Fun 93
    Do Unto Others 95
    Don't Take Yourself Too Seriously 96
    EXERCISE: Keeping Account of Your Abilities 99

Chapter Seven: It's All in Your Head—MINDSET ... 101
    How Do I Develop a Growth Mindset? 103
    Working on Your Growth........................... 104
    Replace Negative with Positive...................... 105
    Practice Makes Perfect, or Almost Perfect............. 106
    Learn to Love People Again 107
    Eight Tips to Feel Like Caring Again 112
    EXERCISE: Foster Your Growth Mindset 115

Chapter Eight: A Personal Growth 90-Day Plan 117
    Your Journal—The First Thirty Days................. 118
    Your Vision Board—The Second Thirty Days 121
    Sharing Your Journey—The Third Thirty Days.......... 125
    EXERCISE: 30-, 60-, & 90-Day Growth Plan........ 129

Chapter Nine: Your Amazing Story 131
    New Life After the Brokenness of Burnout.............. 137

Acknowledgments 139

About the Author 141

Books by Don Womble 143

Foreword by
Master Coach LaKendra Smalley

As the founder and owner of The Global Life Coach Training and Entrepreneur Institute, I have been immersed in the world of mental and behavioral health my entire professional career. My journey has led to the creation of a distinguished mental & behavioral health life coaching school in 2010, where we train and employ life coaches, focusing on behavioral health and serving underserved and underprivileged communities. This dedication stems from a profound understanding of leadership's highs and lows and the path to personal growth.

In *Leadership Burnout and Recovery*, Coach Don Womble takes us on a transformative journey through the challenges of burnout, leading us toward healing and renewal with wisdom and empathy. As someone who has faced similar trials in leadership and personal life, I see this book as not just a source of hope but a practical guide to recovery and growth.

Why trust me on this voyage? My experiences mirror those depicted in Coach Don Womble's book, marked by times of feeling lost and broken. Throughout each chapter, he speaks directly to our innermost challenges, addressing the doubts and questions that often plague us in difficult times.

In Chapter's 1 and 2, "I Am Lost and Broken," Coach Womble doesn't merely recognize our struggles; he affirms them, setting the stage for self-discovery, a journey with which I am intimately acquainted.

Chapter 3's exploration of painful anchors like betrayal, isolation, and addiction resonates with anyone who has endured self-imposed trials. It reminds us that our darkest moments are not the end but the start of transformation.

"Forgive the Pain Away" in Chapter 4 articulates a vital truth. Forgiveness, of others and ourselves, is essential in healing. Coach Womble's insights into resentment, guilt, and blame are transformative and poignant.

Chapters 5 and 6 highlight the role of habits and accountability in recovery. In my coaching career, I've witnessed how consistent, small actions and owning our responsibilities can prevent us from falling into despair.

Chapter 7, "It's All in Your Head," underscores the power of mindset. Developing a growth mindset, as Coach Womble explains, is crucial for overcoming obstacles and embracing new beginnings.

The personal growth plan in Chapter 8 exemplifies Coach Womble's dedication to practical solutions. It's a roadmap that I fully endorse for anyone on a path to rebuild themselves.

In summary, *Leadership Burnout and Recovery* is more than a book; it's a crucial guide for those struggling with burnout. It's a narrative of change that I, Master Coach LaKendra, am honored to introduce to you. As you read, remember that you are not alone in this journey. You are on the path to writing a new, remarkable chapter in your life.

Warm regards,
Master Coach LaKendra Smalley
Founder, The Global Life Coach Training and Entrepreneur Institute (GIC&E Inc)

INTRODUCTION

Burnout is the best at camouflaging itself, but there are many sneaky warning signs. Yes, I like to call them burnout identifiers.

Have you ever found yourself:
- Overwhelmed?
- Drained?
- Having problems sleeping well?
- Experiencing a loss of joy?
- Giving decreased job performance?
- Indulging in harmful habits?
- Apathetic to things that normally brought happiness?
- Having feelings of guilt, shame, or failure?
- Feeling powerless?
- Feeling paranoid?

If you're experiencing burnout, then this book can help you heal and go on to be an even better, stronger leader. Burnout, particularly leadership burnout, results from constant stress and anxiety over an extended period of time and gives its victim a sense of fatigue, disenchanted loss, and disillusionment while causing an emotional withdrawal from work, family, and friends. If burnout remains untreated, a mental breakdown can be on the horizon.

I was the senior leader in a midsize organization when one day I was being abnormally quick-tempered with one of my staff members; I was unusually emotional and quite unreasonable. A couple of her coworkers nearby observed my irregularity. Shortly following the incident, one of my associates approached me in the hall and simply said, "Don, are you all right?"

It was as if a distant light began to illuminate my mind and emotions through the fog of my disillusionment. I wanted to either scream or cry, but instead, I looked at my associate and said, "No, I am *not* all right!" That was the moment I knew that I needed help.

Burnout happens to leaders in all professions. Carey Nieuwhof, a best-selling author, the pastor of a megachurch, and a former attorney, suffered burnout in 2006. He admonishes and encourages leaders from all walks of life to observe their fatigue and be aware of the dark place in life where it seems like they have lost control. He notes that diagnosing burnout is important, but working on the journey to recover is of even more importance. Carey reminds all of us that burnout recovery is not an instant fix. He said it took him six months to move from crisis to functional and then another year to get from 60 to 80 percent normal. It was another three to four years for him to feel 100 percent like himself again.[1]

Burnout affects everyone—employees and leaders. No one is exempt from this painful plight. When your inner drive launches you into the role of leadership, you are quickly saddled with new and momentous responsibilities. And when your head rises above the crowd, you will become a target for ridicule, slander, disappointment, lies, betrayal, and misunderstanding—and the list continues. There will always be someone envious of your life and craving your position at work. Ambition, self-motivation,

---

[1] Nieuwhof, Carey. 2016. "How I Recovered from Burnout: 12 Keys to Finding Your New Normal." Carey Nieuwhof.

and the desire to lead others can promote you into an amazing career and life, but while on your journey to the top, it is imperative to embrace the truth that being a leader comes with monumental challenges stacked on top of the usual ups and downs of everyday life. Also keep in mind that you are not a superhero. More will be expected of you, and not everyone will agree with your decisions and/or your leadership style.

Why Should You Trust Me?

Since I was sixteen, I have been in leadership. It began with my first job as a paperboy. Please don't laugh; I'm serious. I had a couple of guys who worked for me, and my experience in leading others expanded from there. At the ripe old age of eighteen, I was awarded a sales position by winning a contest that consisted of learning store products, organizing merchandise, replicating my responsibilities with new employees, and weekly sales for a six-month period. Just before I turned nineteen, I married my high-school sweetheart and then we worked together to survive while paying my way through college. As our church pastor asked my young bride and me to superintend the church's middle school youth ministry, leadership skills came into play again. This leadership position consisted of about seventy-five seventh and eighth graders and ten adults to assist as we ministered to these young people.

I have been an entrepreneur, starting and owning my own business, and a senior project manager for a national construction company. My position included leading contractors and crews to recreate merchandise venues for some of the largest retailers in the United States. In one of the nonprofit organizations in which I served, I was twenty-one years into my role as CEO when I began the broken journey, experiencing a significant burnout with a mental breakdown. I know what it's like to lead a midsize organization and become "broken" and "trapped," like a bear (I'm physically strong, don't forget it) roaming its habitat only to find that some humans had set a metal trap for the beast's demise.

At the time, I was unaware of my plight. My duration in this position had been highly stressful since day one. A leader always fights stress and anxiety. It is to be expected, just part of the position. That's why we make the big bucks, correct?

I am reminded of a story I heard Zig Ziglar tell. He said, "Do you know how to boil a frog?" He explained that when you place a frog in a pan of boiling water, the frog immediately jumps out. However, if the frog is placed in a pan of cold water, things can turn out differently. The burner under the pan must be turned hotter gradually, and this will eventually boil the frog to death because the slowly rising temperature allows an ongoing sense of false security for the frog.

Just to have a clear understanding, I am not suggesting anyone should attempt to boil a frog, but the concept of gradually boiling to death is a good analogy because burnout happens slowly, creeps up with its own veil of false security.

When anyone becomes a burnout sufferer, there is a loud soul cry. One's inner self begins making desperate distress calls, like sending out an SOS. Save my Overworked Soul. To the burned-out, emotionally bankrupt individual, the deafening cry of the soul is loud within but silent on the outside. When I suffered burnout and would speak to someone about my unrest, it was always as though no one could understand me. Deep within there was always a silent request that I yearned to speak out, but I did not know how. Living in a daze deadened my emotions, and I became inhibited in my fifty shades of numbness.

I understand the agony and desperation of leading and being broken, experiencing the pain of burnout. I have lived it and come out the other side wanting to help as many others fare better as possible! I know that living life in this frame of mind feels dangerous, lonesome, and treacherous, and that you need someone who understands, which is why you picked up this book. Being burned out and hurting is why you will continue reading and gathering food for your soul.

My heart desires to add some hope to your life. I guarantee there are answers for your inner cry, and this book can help you find them. I look forward to the day when you contact me and say, "Don, I was burned out too, but now I am not."

Unfortunately, my burnout went untreated for a substantial amount of time, and the lack of treatment and severity of fatigue led to reducing my tenure. That doesn't have to happen to you. I want to help you navigate this journey so you can recover as soon as possible. I will tell you the truth, and not in mixed-up jargon but rather in real-life terminology while sharing how I found healing from the brokenness of burnout. If you allow me, I will not just be the captain of our ship but will also work alongside you as we sail together on this emotional and mental wholeness journey.

The Voyage

The emotional and physical burnout pit of despair is not only challenging to define but even more perplexing to climb out of. I want to sail with you through the pit of despair and then cruise over to the island of purpose together. The sea will be treacherous at times, and we will become weary. But the prize of discovering your island of relief, freedom, and fulfillment, of answering your SOS, will make the expedition worth it.

In this book, we will break down what burnout can do to anyone, especially those in any leadership capacity, and discuss:

- How to realize and admit feeling burned out and that there is hope for wholeness again.

- The voyage of self-discovery and self-identity.
- The anchors that hold leaders back and how to pull them up.
- To all that is good, there are enemies. We will note the enemies and then, like a surgeon with a purpose, discover the ways to gain freedom from them.
- Having a healthy mind is imperative for enjoying life and growing. Recognizing and being purposeful with healthy habits will guarantee prolonged emotional freedom and growth.
- Learning ways to have accountability is the key to a successful life.
- Since it's all in our heads, we will establish the pathway to a mindset of growth.
- Planning is a pattern of successful people, and a 30- to 90-day growth plan will add a practical perspective to personal growth.
- Reflecting and learning mixed with fun and growth are a proven path to mental and emotional wholeness.

Following each chapter, you will find exercises and/or worksheets that give you the opportunity to consider and implement the material that has been provided in the chapter.

While the principles provided in this writing are primarily for the burned-out to regain mental wholeness, you and I can practice these same teachings to prevent burnout or stop it in its early stages. We will learn how to let go of the things that have us tangled and destined for defeat, how to let go of our anchors and sail forward into a successful and purposeful life of happiness.

These are not only words. I promise to give you a successful pattern you can emulate to prevent and/or recover from burnout.

And I know it is a successful pattern because this approach is how I made it to wholeness again. When I arrived with emotional clarity and the dullness had been removed, it was like standing on the tip of a mountain peak and seeing life spread out before me as the most beautiful valley imaginable. It had been a couple of decades since I'd found such delight in the fresh breaths of air. It was like watching the flutter of butterflies as they flew suspended over a flower and drank its nectar. Finally, clearness of mind and freedom to dream of exciting days were once again possible.

I wish to lead you through a series of emotions, decisions, and realizations that spurred my gradual healing to total health. Attend closely, with your eyes, mind, and emotions grounded in the truth that healing occurs one day at a time. I'm inviting you to follow me as I lead you like a ship's captain on a voyage of self-discovery and then welcome you to a new and refreshing life.

Chapter One

I Am Lost and Broken

When burnout rocks a person's world, it causes them to doubt and question their identity. Things are not the same as they once were. As much as those around us have noticed something is different, to us, it can feel like there is no time to stop and wonder about such things.

The mindset tends to include these thoughts: *I know who I am. I am a leader, a husband or wife, a single parent or a single person, a supervisor, and an entrepreneur, and I am important to this organization and this team of people. There is no time to get all wrapped up in the emotion of things. There is no time for me to be concerned about my feelings. Sacrifice is the name of the game.*

An important characteristic of being a leader is the drive and ability to keep fighting and prevailing through all the blood, sweat, and tears. There is a sense of being a superhero, of *needing* to be a superhero. Think of the numerous times most of us have said things like, "I've got this," or "I've handled worse than this." Leaders naturally wield their superpowers of resilience and decisiveness and are unable to stop being a superhero even when things have become overwhelming or have become more than a human being can carry for longer than we should.

When I was a young child, my mother used a technique on me that I continued to use into my adult life. When she felt as though I was crying but not actually hurt, she used to say to me, "Big boys don't cry." Or perhaps you have heard it put in terms like, "Suck it up, buttercup." This way of thinking tends to follow us into adult life, becoming part of the complexity of the superhero leadership style.

Then too, leadership culture often promotes the idea that there are strong people and weak people and says things like, "If you cannot handle the stress of the job, you are not a fit and we don't need you." Stress, anxiety, and pressure are always a part of life and normal components of most jobs. I once heard someone say, "High-paying jobs have high elements of stress. If you don't want stress, get a low-paying job." But this carte blanche statement does not hold true 100 percent of the time. There are always varying factors—too little, too much, or just enough—in every aspect of life, so blanket statements like these are unrealistic; they cannot possibly be true. No matter how much of a natural-born and highly trained leader one is, the potential for burnout is still present because the demands are not always realistic.

We are *not* superheroes. We are imperfect, flawed human beings with a competitive nature, even though we really need each other. We must have a strong sense of self-identity to be successful in any area of our lives. And the challenging aspect of leadership burnout is to actually stop long enough to look in the mirror of self-identity and realize that we have lost something.

While I was the senior leader in my organization, the board of directors empowered me to lead our multimillion-dollar building program. I interviewed building contractors and chose some of them to give their sales presentation to the directors, and then the board voted on the company to build our project. There was nothing about the decision that was good. Three years and four different contractors later, we were 40 percent over budget when the building was completed. This endeavor sent me to a very dark place. I lost the clarity of my purpose and identity in the quagmire of determination, vision, and duty. I lost myself. I moved from the stage of burnout to clinical burnout and depression. I experienced a nervous breakdown and became unable to function as I once had in my day-to-day life.

My personal psychological and physical healing did not begin until I first learned how to change some things inside of myself. Four distinct steps forward were key in setting myself up for successful recovery and healing: realize it, admit it, have no fear, and trade pride for humility.

Realize It

Just about every person I know has stress in their lives. We have deadlines to meet, uncomfortable conversations with coworkers, lack of communication in the workplace, and occasionally we have teamwork with some on the team do not want to work. So if leaders are natural superheroes with the drive and ability to keep problem-solving through whatever challenges arise, then how do we know when it's really burnout and not just something we are meant to deal with?

Burnout is crafty! Burnout is a slow burner that creeps unexpectantly into a person's life, but there are usually several things that alert us when burnout is dropping anchors that will hold us back.

- Emotional and mental exhaustion
- Lack of personal drive or passion
- Detachment of oneself from thoughts and feelings
- Physical exhaustion

Stress can make a person feel submerged in the moment, but the realization is ever-present that things will get better. Burnout is more like work-related exhaustion that feels like it will never end. A person can feel stuck and without options. Burnout feels hopeless.[2]

Perhaps you are in an early phase of burnout. You may be in the middle or totally psychologically spent already. Wherever you are, I want to be straightforward about this first hurdle you must navigate to emerge victorious from the throes of burnout:

> *Denial is the trickster with which you may have aligned. You have joined arm in arm with the deceiver.*

I know this because this is the way I thought I could ease the pain, and because it's a common theme in my research of other leaders experiencing or having experienced burnout. Burnout is emotional brokenness, and when brokenness occurs, the first instinct is to *deny it*. The problem is someone or something else—it *cannot* be me. One of the most difficult things for most leaders is to *realize* that they "cannot take it anymore."

Think about it. Which leader or entrepreneur wants to say, "Put a fork in me, I'm done?"

Well, it *is* you and me.

> *Denial is a fear response, an internal mechanism that seems to offer a safe place to hide.*

Denial understands you and seeks to shelter you. This hiding place enables you to remain unchanged, protecting you from

---

2 MacLean, Lisa. 2021. "Burned Out or Just Really Stressed? How to Tell the Difference." Henry Ford Health Staff.

the fear of exposing that you have become a burned-out leader and were not a superhero after all.

There are normally feelings of great hesitation preventing leaders from honestly admitting there is a problem or crying out for help. Burnout begins to take control by clouding everything in our minds. Mental fog seems to cover our thinking and inhibits our reasoning and actions. Things that have always been second nature to us become daunting taskwork. We know something is wrong, but we talk ourselves out of accepting it could be coming from within us. But the good news is that you can look in the mirror and choose to be honest, vulnerable, and true to yourself and others.

You are not alone.

There is no need to hide in denial because you're experiencing something most leaders can or will understand very well from their own experiences.

We all tell ourselves lies! Many leaders and entrepreneurs who have recovered from some form of burnout testify that they "lied to themselves." Because each person is so determined and tightly wrapped up in their careers and families, lies seem to protect them from the truth even when signs of burnout are as plain as the nose on their face.

Forbes brings attention to studies regarding leaders burning out at record rates in an article highlighting Development Dimensions International. DDI has been in business since 1970 and worked with more than 75 percent of Fortune 500 companies. They developed a study that is the largest of its kind for their organization.[3]

---

[3] Segal, Edward. 2021. "Leaders and Employees Are Burning Out at Record Rates: New Survey." *Forbes.*

The data is derived from 15,000 leaders and 2,102 human resource professionals representing more than 1,740 organizations in more than twenty-four industries worldwide. Even though most of this survey was taken during the 2020 pandemic, it revealed a problem that had already taken root pre-pandemic. Stress and anxiety take a toll on the lives of everyone to some degree in the workplace. Many people began working remotely at the offset of the pandemic, and some remain and will continue working from home in the future. Few professionals argue that mental and emotional fatigue will always be a factor, especially those 'under the scope' of leadership scrutiny.

The Global Leadership Forecast 2021 indicates that:

- nearly 60 percent of leaders felt the close of the workday used them up, which is a clear indicator of someone burning out; and
- around 44 percent of leaders who felt used up by the close of the workday anticipated changing jobs soon, and 26 percent of these predicted leaving within twelve months. [4]

The Gallup group, in a study performed on 7,500 full-time employees, discovered that 67 percent suffered from burnout in recent years. Twenty-three percent of the individuals claimed they always or often experienced burnout.[5]

The Deloitte survey involving a study of 1,000 full-time employees revealed that 77 percent of these employees experienced burnout.[6]

Lies that we might embrace only cause us to ignore our brokenness, which in turn allows it to worsen and deepen. We say things like:

---

4 https://www.ddiworld.com/global-leadership-forecast-2021
5 Wigert, Ben, and Sangeeta Agrawal. 2018. "Employee Burnout, Part 1: The 5 Main Causes." Gallup.
6 2015. "Workplace Burnout Survey: Burnout Without Borders." Deloitte. https://www2.deloitte.com/us/en/pages/about-deloitte/articles/burnout-survey.html

- This too will pass.
- I'm not ill, just a little tired.
- I don't need to see a counselor or a doctor.
- I can handle anything that comes my way.
- I am a leader, and this is what leaders go through.
- I'm stronger than you think.
- I'm as happy as I've always been.
- I'm not depressed.
- I'm not drinking more than usual.
- I'm not more sarcastic or negative lately.
- I will be fine when this project is completed.
- Once I take a little vacation, I'll be all right.
- The more that I take on, the happier I am.
- I'm okay. I'm just not at the top of my game.
- When people start doing their job, I'll be fine.
- After my vacation, I will be charged up again.
- I haven't changed. You just don't understand me.

The thing every leader must understand is that some of these excuses or lies can have partial truth in them. The part of the lie that we fail to admit too many times is the part that sinks our ship. Our current situation of despair can be the one that takes us down, damages our health, leads us into an inappropriate relationship, or that can change our lives harmfully forever.

The truth though, is that no one can recover until they know what they are recovering from. We must first recognize the signs of burnout and be able to see that we have the symptoms.

Admit It to Quit It

Once a person realizes something is drastically wrong within, they are one step closer to finding the help they need. But what do you have to admit?

The list can be as long or as short as necessary, and necessary means just long enough to make you want to reach out for help. Permit yourself to feel weak. It is all right to feel weak, for it is the beginning of being strong again. A person may feel like admitting weakness is failure and feeble, but it's actually a courageous show of strength to look within and seek to repair, heal, learn, and grow.

Since being a leader does not mean you were born with superpowers and, as a superhero, are not subject to the natural limitations of the human condition, you have to adjust the expectations you have for yourself to truly admit you are burned out and need help to recover and heal. See yourself as the human being you are and realize that you do not need to hide within denial, and then it is time to "tear down the walls."

Following the defeat of Germany in World War II in 1945, the capital of Berlin was divided into four sections. The Americans, British, and French gained control of the western region, and the Soviets gained power over the eastern region. The three western sections united as the Federal Republic, known as West Germany, in May 1949. In October of the same year, the German Democratic Republic was established in East Germany. The East German government erected a wall known as the Berlin Wall in August 1961 to prevent those in the eastern division from escaping to the West. It is estimated that more than 2.5 million people fled to the western side seeking freedom between 1949 and 1961.

The president of the United States, Ronald Reagan, made one of the most famous speeches of the Cold War on June 12, 1987.

With the wall in the background, the president challenged Mikhail Gorbachev, the Soviet leader, to "tear down" the Berlin Wall. Two years later, on November 9, 1989, excited East and West Berlin individuals did break down this huge barrier, and Germany became reunited on October 3, 1990.[7]

With the quote "tear down this wall" being so powerful and "wall" having so many meanings, over time, this phrase turned into a saying that echoes throughout our society still to this day. "Wall" often refers to an inner obstacle, a fortification we build in our minds to protect our emotional health and freedom. The leader who has burned out emotionally and physically will never step into freedom without "tearing down walls" that have subconsciously been built to shield them from the pain they've been experiencing. Juggling a personal life and a professional life can be an uphill struggle, a constant battle. The pressures built up in a leader's psyche often lead to frustration, relationship issues, regret, guilt, hatred, and bitterness. All these walls must be torn down before you can gain emotional and physical freedom.

Each person must determine what they should do to tear down their own walls. I had to separate myself and take a sabbatical. I realize that not everyone can take these measures, but everyone can discern how to get away for at least some period of time, even if only a few days. Take a vacation, use some PTO or even sick leave, and step away to relax and gain a clear focus on your life.

During the first week of my sabbatical, I built a fence in my backyard while unknowingly removing bricks from my inner wall. Each day for five or six days, I began early in the morning and went outside. The crisp September air was fresh and invigorating. I purchased the supplies, developed my work plan

---

[7] History.com editors. 2022. "President Reagan Challenges Mr. Gorbachev to 'Tear Down This Wall.'" A&E Television Networks.

for the day, and began digging, then planting posts. After I built wooden frames, I installed the fence planks. That first week was wonderful for me. As I worked, I felt as though I was accomplishing something that I could see developing into a finished project. I enjoyed God's beautiful sky and watching the birds fly as squirrels jumped from tree limb to tree limb. The occasional bark of a dog and a motorcycle or vehicle noise was refreshing to me. For the first time in months or maybe years, I looked forward to getting up, getting dressed, eating breakfast, and starting my day by going outside and doing something constructive with my hands.

Some might say that symbolically, I unclogged the pipes or the drain. Yes, that's right, I unclogged my foggy mind to think clearly once again, and it had been such a long time since I had a transparent mind. Little did I realize that this small outdoor project was the beginning of my footsteps to mental health renewal. This burned-out man, this broken soul, was on his way to taking positive strides toward regaining a life of freedom and wholeness.

It felt so right and so good that I must encourage you to "Tear down this wall!"

To whom does a leader admit brokenness?

- Yourself
- Your spouse or significant other
- Your parent
- Your family
- Your doctor, psychologist, psychiatrist, counselor, coach
- Your pastor or spiritual leader
- Your best friend
- Your accountability groups
- Your boss or a co-owner

Most likely, other people around you have already noticed your symptoms and are aware that something about you is amiss. The people who love and care for you want to come through for you, but they have no idea how, and we all know you can't tell someone such things. Pushing the issue with someone struggling could make things worse. People have to hit realization on their own first to be open to doing anything about it.

When admitting your condition:

- Be completely honest and open. No shortcuts or half-truths.
- Be clear and specific without giving all the gross details unless you speak to professional help.
- Take responsibility for your ailment—take the blame.
- Ask for help.
- Accept the help you are given.

Admitting you have burned out is also the time to do some soul-searching. Perhaps you need to take some time away from work. Maybe you require a job change or need to hire someone to assist you in doing your job. Understand that you are at a dead end with doing everything exactly the same as before burnout set in. It is imperative that you open up and coordinate with your life partner and/or employer. It is now time to make a simple plan that will put your well-being first so that you can heal and lead again.

Have No Fear

Franklin D. Roosevelt is known for a famous statement recorded in his first inaugural address on March 4, 1933. The president said, "So, let me assert my firm belief *that the only thing we have to fear is fear itself.*"[8]

---

8 "FDR'S First Inaugural Address." 2021. History Matters. https://historymatters.gmu.edu/d/5057%20/

What does his statement mean? By saying that we don't need to be afraid of anything other than being afraid, Roosevelt was challenging the people of the United States to be calm because all the details of the current dilemma would be worked out. If people were to panic, then matters would certainly be worse.

Fear weaves itself into our lives more and more as we slip into denial of our emptiness and lack of power to overcome the symptoms of burnout. And even after admitting you need to heal and avoid burnout because you're not a superhero, fear will arise time and again. It is nourished by the devil in the details that distracts us from the big picture of what is within our control, what is within our responsibilities, what is within our abilities and limitations. Leverage your fears as reminders to plan and follow through, but never allow them to be an inhibiting factor for acting responsibly.

Let's be honest. Fear usually relates to the unknown. We fear 'What if?' because we can't see into the future and be sure, and then this uncertainty breeds imaginary monsters we might have to face and convinces us to avoid risking it. Fear of 'What if' is usually the sea serpent that lifts its head and brings debilitating anxiety into a person's life, and it attacks when a person is at their most vulnerable, making their mind run wild with all manner of what-ifs.

Here are some of the natural fears most common when considering letting our wall come down:

1. What should I do now?
2. What will others think?'
3. What if I'm embarrassed?
4. What if I lose money?
5. What if I lose business?
6. What if I lose my job?
7. What if my reputation is harmed?
8. What if people misunderstand me?
9. What if I never feel whole again?
10. What if there are consequences?

Sounds familiar, doesn't it?

I have two words to help you work through your fear. Ready? Here they are:

Stop it!

You became a leader to begin with by stepping over your fears. You moved into leadership with a passion for being great at what you do. So *confront* your fears. Every leader who wants to recover from burnout and leave behind the 'fried' mindset must defeat their 'What if?' fears. These what-ifs are a complete waste of your valuable time and emotional energy.

Did you know that only a small percentage of fears actually ever come true?

Some members of the Department of Psychology from the University of Pennsylvania studied twenty-nine patients with generalized anxiety disorders. Over a period of ten days, the individuals recorded their worries and then they monitored their fears for the next thirty days. The findings revealed that 91.4 percent of anticipated worries did not come true. Most of the participants did not have a single worry come true in that period of one month.[9]

I suggest that you and I learn from this model. Here is my takeaway:

Don't overthink it.

Every one of us deals with fear at some level, which implies that even though we may feel alone, we are not like a single vessel in the ocean. Most of our fears do not come true, which suggests that most of our fears are irrational. Now we can move on to

---

9 LaFreniere, Lucas S. and Michelle G. Newman. "Exposing Worry's Deceit: Percentage of Untrue Worries in Generalized Anxiety Disorder Treatment." *Behav Ther*. 2020 May; 51(3): 413-423.

the fourth step of embarking on the journey to recovery, which is actually a familiar partner with fear.

Trade Your Pride for Humility

Another emotion that partners with fear, almost as if together they are a two-headed monster, is pride. There is seldom anything wrong with a sense of pride in our achievements, but an overinflated sense of pride that puts ego first can cripple our ability to look beyond ourselves and inhibit us from admitting our weaknesses so we can turn them into strengths. This type of pride is self-centered, looking out for personal good to the detriment of others, but also stopping us from calling out for help where help is needed. Sometimes I imagine pride as a pit that has been dug to catch a wild animal, but instead of the animal falling into the pit, the person who dug the pit falls in.

Humility should win the battle over pride. For any one of us to grow in character, humility is the key. Many a leader has fallen because humility was foreign to them. If pride does not submit to humility, then harmful coping mechanisms can easily find their way into our lives to help us deal with what we are not willing to admit or improve within ourselves.

Exercise:
Finding and Fixing Me

Realize It

List all of the negative feelings you're experiencing that have you overwhelmed, out of control, done, and burned out.

Admit It to Quit It

Classify each one as most related to your personal, professional, or family life.

Have No Fear

List out the fears keeping you from addressing burnout in your life, with the people affected and/or in a position to notice.

Add the worst-case scenario for each fear. What if each of those fears came true?

Add a YES or NO at the beginning of each item to indicate if each fear is likely to come true or not, being realistic and honest with yourself. Then look back over the list and see if there is really anything to fear at all.

Trade Your Pride for Humility

What could you accomplish by asking for help with each item in your Realize It list? Could it make things worse? Or, more likely, how much better could things be?

Chapter Two

What Am I Supposed to Do?

Who are you? This breakthrough has nothing to do with a job title, position, or business ownership. Who are you as a *person*?

Ask yourself:

> Where am I with the first four steps to burnout recovery, realizing it, admitting it, having no fear, and exchanging humility for pride? What is my plan to obtain mental clarity and wholeness? These thoughts cannot be answered immediately, but they are essential to discovering our true selves.

Discover Your True Self

Who we truly are includes all of our memories, experiences, relationships, beliefs, and feelings. So much of this complete psychological makeup becomes mixed-up, confused in our thinking when we burn out because we are thinking through a murky filter. This skewed way of thinking will affect so much of our life, including our relationships. Recently, I worked with a client who had just become aware of his burnout. In one of our first sessions, he shared that because of his mental state, he feels he has let everyone down in his life. He was disappointed in himself because he believed that he had disappointed everyone else.

Quite often, at least some of our personal identity has been forced upon us by family, society, peers, and the like, and this is a major stressor that may be chipping away at everything else without our even realizing it. A forced identity is a false identity that makes us subconsciously role-play our life. It doesn't fit us, who we really are, and so we struggle to navigate everything, like wearing the wrong size shoes and trying to run a marathon. Identity and expectations are not the same. Anyone living their life with the focus on trying to please someone else is living according to what they assume to be expected at the expense of who they are.

Once you discover, or rediscover, your identity, you'll naturally want to do something to better align yourself. I have a friend who says, "Do something even if it's wrong!" Well, I wouldn't go that far, *or would I?* This can be extremely difficult, but once you commit to doing something, it will become easier to figure out what to do.

Most important, don't stand still. It's not in you to stand still—you are a leader of others and not one to stand in the background. This does not mean anyone should immediately jump back into the leadership role. Movement and growth should progress slowly to truly be progress. You're making a move right now just by reading this book. Keep moving forward through the pages as we map out each next step.

Build Self-Respect

*"Respect your efforts, respect yourself.
Self-respect leads to self-discipline.
When you have both firmly under your belt,
that's real power."*
– Clint Eastwood.[10]

Self-identity and self-respect are closely related, though many people often do not think of self-respect until they have lost it. To maintain your true self-identity, it is imperative to build self-respect.

Essentially, self-respect is a form of self-care. Self-respect is loving yourself and treating yourself with care and is the result of staying true to your values and not being willing to compromise. It means believing that you deserve love, consideration, and opportunities like everyone else. Every human being has flaws. We all have blemishes, bruises, and scars. Comparing yourself with others will only make you feel worse, like you're not good enough, and will minimize your achievements, but the more you engage in behaviors consistent with your beliefs and values, the more you'll feel fulfilled and confident.[11]

I want to give you some steps that I used to discover my true self and rebuild my self-respect following a four-year major burnout. Though not in any particular order, this advice can serve as a guide to developing short-term and long-term targets for continuous improvement that you can structure to fit your unique needs more specifically. Many of these concepts are accepted by professionals in the medical field.[12]

---

10 Eastwood, Clint. 2010. "The Man Quote: Clint Eastwood." Dysonology.
11 Casabianca, Sandra Silva and Kaitlin Vogel. 2022. "How to Regain Your Self-Respect and Why It Matters." PsychCentral.
12 Raypole, Crystal. 2021. "Burnout Recovery: 11 Strategies to Help You Reset." Healthline. Medically reviewed by Deborah Weatherspoon, PhD, MSN.

Steps to wholeness following burnout:
- Get a health checkup.
- Develop an easy daily plan of activities.
- Go to bed early and rise and shine early.
- Have some personal quiet time. Use this for focus, meditation, and spiritual growth.
- Be careful what you eat—it is advised to not eat heavy foods for a while.
- Do some morning stretches to release stress and tension.
- Prepare a simple 'today to-do list.'
- Get fresh air.
- Take proper vitamins.
- Check in with yourself sometime after lunch to see how you're thinking.
- Read books that you like and books that help you grow as a person.
- Enjoy family and friends.
- Plan special outings.
- Don't feel guilty for putting yourself first. You are healing and doing what is best for you right now.
- Don't allow your fears, anxieties, or others to dictate your actions.
- Remember, you've got this!

Life Goes On

It took around three years following my resignation from the organization to obtain mental wholeness. Even today, I have flashbacks as I relive some mental anguish from moments that left a mark on my mind. But life has gone on, and it will for you too.

Before I resigned from the organization, there was so much to consider. I had just reached the twenty-five-year mark as the leader. Think with me through this. Being with an organization, a group of people and a community, for *one-quarter of a century* is an accomplishment, right? It's either bitter, sweet, or bittersweet. For my wife, children, and me, it was bittersweet. All three of our children grew up during this period. This was all they knew. Their dad was a leader, and he was well-respected in the community. We knew many people, and many people knew us.

As I worked through my what-ifs, those questions caused something to change in me that I had not given attention to before. Trying to find solutions led me to the questions, 'Who am I?' and 'What is my identity?'

One morning I began thinking and praying, desperate to sort out what my true identity was, and then I asked myself:

- Is my identity being the CEO of this organization?
- Is my identity being the husband of my wife, Kathy?
- Is my identity being the dad of my three children?
- Is my identity being a leader in this community?
- Is my identity being Don, the person I was purposed to be?

It seemed so crazy asking myself these questions, but they ended up being the breakthrough questions that led to the defining moment for me. I realized that I had placed my identity in my *job position*, my *title*, along with my *leadership within the community*. Therefore, if I resigned, I would be *losing my identity*!

Somewhere along the way, my identity had become wrapped up in my professional position. My thought development was part of my deep-down heart issue. Somewhere, I'd lost it, and somehow, I had become my job. Then I understood why I took everything so personally. I was beginning to recognize why I could not mentally heal. Things were coming together, showing me why I was hurting so deeply inside. The light bulb switched on when I had discussions with people I felt close to. I would cry within, wanting to scream at the top of my lungs, "Help me!" It became apparent that they could not hear my cry, or perhaps they did not know what they could say to help me.

It took losing my identity to find my identity.

This last statement was unveiled in all its simplicity. I was given the breakthrough that I needed. Walking through the questions, I began to answer them aloud to myself, which went as follows:

- My identity is *not* being the CEO of this organization.
- My identity is *not* being the husband of my wife Kathy.
- My identity is *not* being the dad of my three children.
- My identity is *not* being a leader in this community.

The fifth question gave me the answer. No, I was not the person I was supposed to be. Rather, I had become convoluted in the quagmire of burnout.

Is my identity being Don, the person I was purposed to be? And the answer shouted a big affirmative, Yes! This was as simple as the nose on my face, but I could not see it.

I accepted that I wanted to live out my identity in being the person I was purposed to be and went on a personal quest. That journey led me to search deep within, giving me time to heal. I read encouraging things daily. I began spending about ten minutes journaling each morning, writing out whatever was on my mind. The next day, I reviewed the previous day's journal and then wrote for another ten minutes to record my thoughts that day. This habit became customary for about a year. I learned a great deal about *Don* and grew in my personhood. Life was not about a job or a position or a title. Life was about learning and being who I was while enjoying my family.

I got a new job and served on Sundays at church. This sabbatical gave me the chance to clear my mind and look forward to the things that Don was supposed to be or do.

First, I wrote a list of five things I could see myself doing for the remainder of my working life. After making the list, I looked at it every morning and thought about it and prayed about it. If prayer isn't your thing, you can still follow through with all the other parts if you make such a list. Now, get this—my list of five things was prioritized in order of my submission and availability. I thought I was willing to do any of those five things, but as the list went from one to five, my resistance also grew. As time lapsed, some things became humorous in relation to other items on my list.

I wholeheartedly believe that every person has a unique plan for their life whether they know it or not. As I crafted my list, I remained flexible because, as we all know, life often gives us detours. As I lay out how all of this worked for me, of course we both know it will work differently for you, and so I want to give you a pattern that you can use to make your own list. The items on my list were about doing ministry and serving people in some shape or fashion.

For around nine months, I researched and prayed about the type of ministry I could lead. Here is my list of five things written down according to my desires from first to last:

1. Get a marketplace job, go to a church, and serve in some capacity on Sunday.

2. Serve as a staff pastor in some church bi-vocationally. (That means having a secular job and a church pastor's job part-time.)
3. Become a foreign missionary. My wife and I even applied and interviewed with a major denomination to serve as foreign missionaries. We decided to withdraw our application before going before the national mission board for various complicated reasons.
4. Become the lead pastor of a church somewhere. That church would have to be the perfect fit to not be crossed off my list.
5. Be a part of planting a new church somewhere but not be the lead pastor.

I remained uncertain about my future for some time, focusing on each day and placing boundaries in my life to never return to a burned-out frame of mind. Then, as I was embracing my newfound identity, something occurred that led to a life-changing experience for me.

Two friends of mine who did not know each other had been consistently pestering me about starting a church. I was not ready for that. I was still working on healing myself, so their meeting each other was a better solution. I arranged a dinner party to introduce them, and we had a wonderful dinner and what felt like a couple of hours of enjoyable conversation. I did not talk much that night, preferring to kind of be a fly on the wall and listen. I wanted them to talk and share their thoughts and dreams of starting a new church.

After feeling ready to leave for a good while, finally, I motioned for my wife to start getting ready to head home. Before I made my move to excuse us, one of these friends asked if he could say something to me. I will call him George. Despite how late it was, I agreed to listen.

George said, "Don, you may get uncomfortable after hearing me say some things on my mind. You can get up and leave if you wish, or you may want to punch me in the face."

Of course everyone wanted to chuckle, but they were as unsure of what he was going to say as I was. Then he explained that he felt compelled to disclose to me how it seemed like the entire evening was not about any of them. The night had been exclusively for me. He also shared some things about me that were true as he spoke about where he thought I was in my life and what it would take to move me into the place I was looking for. This was an unusual moment for me, listening to this gentleman share his discernments about my life. I think he talked for about thirty minutes.

When he was finished, I thanked him and the others and my wife and I promptly left their house and got into our car. After sitting in the car for a few moments, I started it up and slowly buckled my seat belt. Truthfully, I just wanted to disappear. I felt as though the nighttime stars and the moon were spotlighting me. I sensed the people at my friend's house were all peering through the window curtains to watch my next move. It was as though I had frozen. Strangely, I did not want to look at my wife and was hoping she would forget that we were in the car together. I anticipated it was coming. My wife knew me so well that she would not be able to keep herself from speaking to me. I began to perspire while the silence became louder and louder. And then it happened!

My wife remarked, "Well, it sounded like that man had your number tonight."

I did not like what she had to say, nor what the man had said.

I wanted to be angry with my wife for having the audacity to make such a judgmental statement, but I knew she was correct.

I was just too confused, cranky, and conflicted to discuss it. I slowly glanced at her and said, "Yes, he did," as I placed the gear shift in the drive position and left that place. My wife and I quickly commenced our short thirty-minute drive home in silence. I was upset and did not want to talk, something which she had intuitively sensed.

Unknown to me, the entire evening marked the beginning of a personal breakthrough in my life. The event had begun as casually as expected, and the evening had ended with uncertainty and confusion. Little did I or my wife know how our lives were about to drastically change. I will finish that story later in this book, but for now, there is a powerful thing I hope lands in your heart. When you allow others to speak words of truth, love, and perspective into your life, you can learn, grow, and change. Do not be bullheaded like I am at times. Be an open vessel waiting to be filled with truth, knowledge, and wisdom from others who are brave enough to give you tough love and speak directly into your life.

To progress in your journey of healing from burnout, you have to become unstuck from your current lost state of mind so you can begin to think creatively again. Being unstuck means focusing on different and new things that can have a positive impact rather than focusing on the burned-out feelings and negative voices plaguing you from before. Creativity opens an innovative and fresh frame of thought. Being creative allows you to dream again. You can begin to consider the possibility of good things that could be part of your purpose in life. As you move through your quagmire of confusion and out of the dark haze, a glimmer of hope can arise. As you heard in my story, I needed someone from the outside to initiate that trigger in my mind. I had fallen into such a deep emotional pit, I needed someone to reach down and help pull me up to begin thinking with visionary insight again. What triggers your *aha* moment may be different, but be open to receiving the signal so you don't miss it.

Here are some ideas that I found incredibly helpful from my research on how to find yourself when you feel a loss of self-identity:

- Go to a quiet place and just think positive thoughts.
- Listen to your body and rest.
- Consider stretching your comfort zone—try dreaming again.
- Do something different—take a day trip or a weekend retreat.
- Look for a mentor that you can trust and glean from.
- Sit down and write whatever is on your mind—try it seven days in a row.
- Do something that you love to do, either simple or big.
- Read a book or listen to a book that will challenge you and cause you to grow.
- Be bold and ask for help.[13]

Be Authentically You

Once you have found your identity, it's time to become you again! There is so much that is fake and phony in our world that it is always refreshing to come in contact with people who are genuinely themselves.

Because we all have unique personalities, it takes a leap of faith to show ourselves at the risk of revealing our vulnerability, so it can be difficult for some. In general, I have found that the world craves transparency in friendships, relationships, organizations, churches, and our government, so it makes sense to

---

[13] Serf-Walls, Lamisha. 2017. "7 Tips to Find Yourself When You're Feeling Lost." Huffpost.

extrapolate that there is more reward than risk in being authentic. Authenticity is important to me, just like it is to so many of you. My family means the world to me. My wife and I have purposed to live authentically before our children their entire lives. Now, they all have families of their own, but it's refreshing to hear each of them from time to time express the value of our vulnerability and transparency around them. There are few things that bless my heart more than hearing one of our adult children mention to someone else, "Dad and Mom are the same at church or in the public eye as they are at home."

As I live out my true identity, I have discovered that I am free to live and free to be me, which in turn allows me to enjoy relationships with others more deeply than ever before. I am far from perfect, but this freedom liberates me to be real, to be who I am in public just as I am at home, no longer bound by any factors in my identity that were forced on me by environment or society or carried forward from the inexperience of my youth.

Authenticity makes us the best version of ourselves, and the public life of a leader is extremely important. When leaders feel broken following burnout, public life can be challenging. You may bump into work associates and old friends who will want to catch up on the past in a few short minutes. But if you are dealing with physical or mental brokenness, you may try to avoid all such instances. That is normal, and that is okay.

There are many things to keep in mind as you begin to venture into the public.

You need to get out. It's healthy for you.
If your burnout shifted to depression, you would battle within to stay home and out of public view. Some of that is healthy but only to a point. There is a time to go outside, go to the park, see a movie, or take a walk with a loved one around the block or inside the local mall. Your mental health begs you to get out

and be among people. If your struggle prevents you from going out, you should see a professional who can advise you regarding public life.

Everyone is not looking at you.
You may battle some instincts of being paranoid. Just enjoy whoever is with you and don't feel that you must look around. Be aware of your surroundings, but do not try to look for people you recognize. I do not want to be offensive, but you must realize, *"It's not all about you."* Everyone is not looking at you. They are not thinking bad things about you. Most people don't have the time or the inclination to focus on others this way, if you really think about it. Because you have so much of yourself in your mind, you might be tempted to think they are looking at you and thinking negatively about you. But you are not their focus, and they have no idea what you are dealing with to even be interested. Shake off that paranoid feeling. It is unhealthy, and it is untrue.

Be humble, with no chip on your shoulder.
Since you want your life to add value to someone or something, stay humble and be kind. When a person says something that may seem offensive, just disregard it. Your emotions may be tender and easily offended because you're dealing with burnout. What wouldn't normally bother you likely will during this challenging time, so be aware of that and disregard it, don't let it make you feel worse. We have all seen someone who seems to be waiting for anyone to offend them so they can give them a piece of their mind, which usually is a big scene that just makes them look bad to the casual observer and accomplishes nothing.

Think before you speak.
Because we are all different and our emotions have been injured by anxiety overload, be conscious that your kindness and consideration shines. Remember that we reap what we sow. If we

want to be the recipient of other people's love and kindness, we should purposely show love and kindness to others. My mother used to tell me to think three times before speaking when you are hurt or offended. This has proven to be healthy advice for me, allowing me to avoid saying things I would regret and instead take a hard look at my way of thinking in the moment.

Do unto others...

Yes, treat others the way you want to be treated. When you want to just rip into someone with words of not so much wisdom, put yourself in their shoes for a moment. None of us know what the other person experienced that day. Perhaps something horrible transpired in their life, making them less themselves such that they said or did something hurtful. Give people a break; give them a margin for error because they deserve it.

We need to keep in mind that life is all about people, and always presenting our authentic selves is what we and everyone who deals with us deserves in any kind of relationship.

I am excited for you and your discovery of your *true self*, and in the next chapter, we will dig a little deeper. Sometimes surgery is required to achieve healing, but you're in good hands. I have a great deal of experience on this journey to wholeness and healing.

Exercise:
Learn and Grow

1. Map out your steps to wholeness. Here are some ideas to get you started:

   - Get a health checkup.
   - Prepare a simple 'today to-do list.'
   - Go to bed early and rise and shine early.
   - Have some personal quiet time for focus, meditation, and spiritual growth.
   - Dietary changes.
   - Do some morning stretches to release stress and tension.
   - Get fresh air.
   - Take proper vitamins.
   - Check in with yourself sometime after lunch to see how you're thinking.
   - Read books that you like and books that help you grow as a person.
   - Enjoy family and friends.
   - Plan special outings.
   - Don't feel guilty for putting yourself first.
   - Don't allow your fears, anxieties, and others to dictate your actions.

2. Lose your identity to find your identity. Ask yourself questions like these, based on your current roles:

   - Is my identity being the _____ of this organization?
   - Is my identity being the spouse/partner/friend of my _____?
   - Is my identity being the parent of _____?

- Is my identity being a _____?
- Is my identity being *me*, the person I was purposed to be?

3. Begin to keep a journal about how your life will go on. And, yes, every day.
4. Tomorrow read the previous day's journal and write a new journal for that day.
5. Work on mental healing. Grow in who you are and who you're supposed to be.
6. Make your list of possible things you have a passion for doing.

You may be staying with your job or business. If you are, make a list of new ways to take care of business while caring for yourself instead of going back to the 'same ole way' because you will get the 'same ole thing'—burnout!

Chapter Three

Painfully You—The Anchors

As you approach and navigate burnout, you may employ coping mechanisms that can anchor you deeper and deeper in burnout, making it difficult for you to move forward on your journey. As the captain of your ship in life, you'll have to decide you want to pull up these anchors or not let them drop to begin with, so they don't weigh you down. This chapter points out how to identify and address several common bad mechanisms that it's easy to lean upon as coping habits when you are burned out. Being aware and avoiding these bad habits will increase your chances to advance in healing.

Self-Imposed Troubles—You Did It

Overachievers have a higher risk for burnout because they take on more and attempt to make up the difference for underperformers. Remember that subconsciously, leaders tend to think they are superheroes. Successful leaders are often self-motivated and self-motivators, doing whatever it takes for the task to be accomplished. However, we should beware. Often, people wake up with burnout owing to self-implosion. It's been said many times that we are our own worst enemy.

It's important to set boundaries so that you don't take on more than you are actually responsible for in your leadership role. Be your authentic self, with boundaries that allow you to fulfill your responsibilities, keep your commitments, and not spend extra time and energy trying to be a superhero.

Over the years, I have known so many people who could not discipline themselves to work out at the gym or monitor their eating habits until an unhealthy medical report was placed in front of them. The doctor says, "Diet and exercise or die," before they act on it. This happened to me thirteen years ago, and I have taken it seriously ever since. Like with any illness, it usually takes the situation becoming severe to prompt making a request for help. Let us not be stubborn but rather be honest with our authentic selves. Self-implosion is the enemy of many leaders.

A person must be honest with themselves and look within, but it can be very insightful to get feedback from others as well. Be brave enough to request transparency from those who are close to you and promise them no retaliation for their loving honesty.

A large segment of my burnout was of the "self-imposed, I did it" variety. I tried to wear too many hats of responsibility and was certain I wore a cape like any self-respecting superhero. Many of the things that transpired in my life were 'humorous in hindsight.' The Urban Dictionary defines 'humorous in hindsight' as "*a situation that, at the moment, is stressful and chaotic.*"[14] It later becomes funny because enough time has passed to realize how ridiculous it was. It feels very real while you're in it, of course, but rest assured that if you follow the advice in this book, you too will be able to look back one day and chuckle about it as you celebrate how much you've grown and improved your life.

---

14 2021. "Humorous in Hindsight." Urban Dictionary.

Betrayal

Betrayal is experienced when trust is broken and can be a form of trauma. The victim is left deeply hurt, shocked, and angry. This destructive breach of trust can show up in so many different forms and will certainly hurt everyone involved. Betrayal fragments relationships at their core and can have long-lasting consequences.

Here are some examples of internal thoughts leaders might experience in their relationships with associates and/or peers that tend to feel like betrayal:

> *I trusted this person with personal information, and now they have used it against me.*
>
> *I can't believe my peers threw me under the bus in yesterday's management meeting.*
>
> *I helped these two employees work out a problem, and now they have joined together to ruin me.*
>
> *I trusted a co-manager with my personal struggles, and now he is making others doubt my work ethic.*
>
> *I have led this project and worked extra hours like no one else, yet my associate has taken credit for it.*
>
> *I have loved and helped a team member, and now they are gossiping about me.*

When we feel betrayed, the natural inclination is to fight back, but this only makes the victim look at fault and certainly doesn't contribute to maintaining professionalism. If a person is naturally insecure, betrayal makes moving forward in a positive way even more difficult.

When various people betray a leader over a period of years, it adds up. Betrayal is certainly an anchor for some people to grow bitter and eventually burn out. Becoming weary of dealing with people's issues and disturbances can lead a person to want to give up. Every leader must find ways to battle betrayal because it will always be just around the corner in most of our lives.

To best overcome betrayal, it works as a 'two-way street.' When it comes to relationships, we should be reminded that they require cultivating. Spending proper and healthy time communicating with others in a respectful manner is essential. When disagreements arise it is wise to be a good listener as well as a good communicator. Sometimes leaders become their own worst enemy by falling short with listening and giving some grace to work associates or subordinates. Bypassing these good people skills can come back to haunt us. When we feel someone has betrayed us, it may be the result of something wrong on our part. By both parties working to resolve issues, we can come to agreements that bring unity. This technique should always be our first objective in seeking resolution when there are conflicts.

However, often recovery can only occur as a 'one-way street.' The one-way street can occur when so much damage has been done that the other party doesn't want to work it out. In some cases, one person is looking for an opportunity to gain status by turning their loyalty to someone else. This is when betrayal becomes a reality.

Practice the following positive steps to overcome the pain of betrayal:

- Accept your part in betrayal or the relationship fiasco.
- If possible, meet with the offender or the offended—perhaps have a moderator.
- If you are the betrayer, seek forgiveness from those you've hurt.

- If you have been betrayed, practice forgiving your offender.
- Say 'I'm sorry.'
- Say 'I forgive you.'
- Determine not to lump all people into the category of your offense.
- See a professional therapist or counselor if you are unable to work through the betrayal.

A leader's first objective must be to attempt resolution in terms that can work for all individuals involved. Do not fool yourself; coming to unity in the workplace is actual work on all of our parts. While many disputes do not work out well, you and I should let go of the disagreement. An attempt has been made to correct the issue. Regardless of the outcome, we must forgive and move forward to complete our task.

Isolation

When people feel overwhelmed, mentally and physically exhausted, the tendency is to withdraw. They often don't feel they are doing their job well. Who wants to be around others when they feel like they are underperforming?

The feeling of not 'pulling your own load' doesn't make anyone want to be part of the crowd. All of these feelings of being disconnected make a person pull away, and less interaction divides people from the team. Loneliness can cause burnout. Loneliness works its way into the fabric of a person's mind. According to the World Health Organization, *burnout is characterized by cynicism, negativism, and an increased desire for mental distancing.*[15]

---

15 Turner, Ashley. 2019. "The World Health Organization Officially Recognizes Workplace 'Burnout' as an Occupational Phenomenon." CNBC.com.

As more people work remotely, less face-to-face contact other than Zoom meetings breeds loneliness. Isolation for most people is never good in the long-term. Some people become so engulfed with self-inducing issues that they still feel lonely even when they are among others. All leaders should watch out for the symptoms of loneliness. There are many ways leaders can prepare themselves to 'stop' retreating when honest evaluation tells them loneliness is on the horizon.

The various ways to react to loneliness as a leader:

- Admit your isolation is an impairment to your well-being.
- Start with small positive steps but take steps to be among others.
- Locate a counselor, coach, or therapist to help you with your tendency to go into isolation.
- Determine to find someone you trust to hold you accountable with healthy actions.
- Begin to actively move into people engagement situations in small ways.

Lack of Self-Care

Often, those in leadership are so consumed with their responsibilities and striving for success that they haven't given enough attention to their own self-care. This is unfortunate. If the vehicle can carry the load, it must have the proper regular inspections for fluids and lubricants and any other appropriate maintenance and repairs. Shouldn't our minds, bodies, and spirits have the same consideration for care as our automobiles, or, ideally, even better consideration?

I know most of the excuses for putting myself way down on the list of priorities:

- I don't have time to worry about myself.
- I'm too busy caring for others.
- I'll take a day or two off when this project is finished.
- I'm happy with the way I am.
- There is no time in my schedule to go to the doctor.
- I can't take the time to be selfish.
- Too many people need me.

Most people will admit that good leaders are not self-absorbed but are *selfless*. The ability to find excuses for placing everyone and everything at the top of the to-do list is as natural as breathing. Doing the natural thing is not always the healthiest.

This is where things must get real. To ignore self-care is to place everything you love and hold dear in jeopardy. Placing a job ahead of health and family will set up even the most intelligent and gifted person for utter ruin. Personal boundaries, along with a keen awareness of what is truly best for oneself, establish a mental and physical hedge of protection that can endure for a lifetime. Each of us should foster such a self-awareness that we recognize our self-care is actually selfless care. After all, how can you help others if you are burned out? You have to take care of the caregiver first to be able to give care to others.

What can be done to move away from the lack of self-care?

- Admit you must take care of yourself.
- Make gradual steps to start taking care of yourself.
- Plan and observe personal time for yourself.
- Schedule time to get away and do nothing but "chill."
- Cancel all excuses.

- Get accountability with someone (perhaps a counselor or coach) you trust to check up on you and get rough with you on your personal care if necessary.
- Commit to keeping personal care at the forefront of your priorities.

Entrapment

The word entrapment is often used as a legal term referring to someone being tricked into committing a crime. But it also means, simply, the "condition of being trapped." It's something leaders can experience from the pressures of life and work, just because of the responsibilities that come with being a leader. You can step into the trap of being tricked by the overwhelming and unachievable goals your job and success brings you. The trap was unnoticed at first. It was camouflaged by dreams, achievement, and money. Then the toil of stress and anxiety becomes a load too heavy for any person to continually bear. As burnout begins to grow in any person's life, a sense of entrapment can also emerge.

I have been in the situation in my work environment in which the overload of anxiety made me feel claustrophobic. The responsibility was mine to ensure that a project was a success or a failure. I had to manage the crews, shipments, store managers, rental equipment, broken supplies, state and city permits, mall managers, security, accounts payable and accounts receivable, and repair of broken trucks while trying to spend time with my family and have time for self-care as well.

This claustrophobic feeling could be compared with being enclosed and locked into a commercial airplane. If this flight is nonstop from Dallas, Texas, to Tokyo, Japan, that means the plane will not land for a long time because it will fly over oceans and continents without any hope of landing for around seventeen hours. A person on this flight who suffers from anxiety attacks because of being claustrophobic must either get drunk (I don't recommend it), take a physician-prescribed sleeping pill, or learn ways to control their anxieties.

Ultimately, job pressure and expectations can rise to a level at which leaders, such as project managers, entrepreneurs, and corporate leaders, must practice self-help methods. Often the anxiety-filled person can step away and creatively do something refreshing. Here are some thought-worthy ideas:

- Get away from the computer.
- Walk out of the cubical, office, warehouse, house, or wherever your surroundings add to your feelings of entrapment.
- Go to the restroom and sit down in a stall and be still.
- Reschedule a meeting if possible.
- Get somewhere, close your eyes, zone out, and meditate or pray.
- Move somewhere private and listen to a song that you like.
- Watch a funny five-minute YouTube video.
- Scan through family photos that are on your phone.
- Use the lunch hour to exercise or take a thirty-minute nap in a safe place.
- Get the assistance of a professional counselor, coach, or therapist.

It will be imperative to learn techniques that help you be in control of your thoughts instead of letting your thoughts control you. There are exercises for this type of mindfulness, and a good counselor or coach can assist. Mindfulness is a wonderful and fulfilling practice, which we will address in a later chapter.

Nasty Secret Addictions

This is the age of *secret addiction*, and leaders are not exempt from being controlled by various harmful addictions. How is it that intelligent people find themselves wrapped in destructive vices? It is much easier than you might think and can happen to anyone. I have come across several clients who had been prescribed medication to ease pain owing to an injury. The prescription drug became an addiction because of prolonged usage, and thus the problem worsened.

Addictions become nasty when they control the individual and ruin their lives, and usually the addict keeps their problem secret for as long as possible. An addiction to something can begin small. It is by the continual practice or indulgence of a habit being given priority over responsibilities that it can become harmful. The addiction grows into a craving, a need, and then dependence on the habit. Starting out, the habit is small, but then it gradually grows out of control, like a snowball rolling downhill. The snowball will eventually build up with snow and become large and too difficult to handle. This is how small habits become large addictions that can derail us from our purpose in life.

Because leaders are human and carrying so much responsibility requires coping mechanisms, they can be vulnerable to drugs or alcohol as a form of escapism. These things seem to bring momentary relief, but the approach will only create more problems. Many leaders who succumb to addiction do not see it coming. The addiction seems to be their friend. But as with everything else, once you realize it, then you can focus on ways to stop it.

Here are some ways to eliminate nasty secret addictions:

- Recognize that you have an addiction.
- Admit this addiction is taking you to a very dark place.

- Find your reason.
- Remove things that trigger the addiction.
- Get help from a professional. This action will also figuratively open the can of worms, but this must be done to find help and healing.
- Visualize being free from the addiction.
- Choose a substitute. Find or develop some creative healthy coping mechanisms to help relieve stress and anxiety.
- Hang out with people who are living the way you want to live.

Addiction is a bad habit or anchor pulling a person down that has forcefully taken both men and women leaders and nonleaders out of the workplace temporarily. The anchor is no respecter of persons, and almost any person can fall victim. Realizing it, admitting it, and fearlessly setting pride aside will position you to overcome addiction and heal so you can move forward.

Infidelity

Infidelity takes out some of the best in leadership. Businesses and nonprofit organizations always experience more infidelity than any will admit.

When a leader's mindset is approaching or enduring burnout, he or she might see the potential for comfort or escape in the temptation of an affair. When symptoms of burnout surface within, you must be conscious of your susceptibility to an inappropriate sexual relationship. A leader might either be married or divorced, engaged or separated, a widow or widower, or perhaps single and not looking for a relationship. In any case, something new can appear exciting and offer the promise of relief from feeling so bad in so many other ways.

With thirty-plus years of experience as a counselor and therapist, specializing in issues related to infidelity, marriage, divorce, and dating, Dr. Bonnie Eaker Weil has stated that all of her adultery patients suffer from this, a "biochemical craving for connection."

Burnout from high stress causes low energy and sleep is last on the list of priorities. Lack of sleep then causes cravings for carbs, sugar, and tasty foods to overcompensate, but both are culprits of a self-medicating adulterous behavior. Other side effects are poor, impulsive decisions or judgment, lack of clarity in the brain, and the like. For success and fidelity in a relationship, adequate sleep and a healthy diet need to be as much of a priority as a daily affirmation and gratitude (*not criticism*) to your partner.

Then Dr. Weil makes this enlightening statement, "Monogamy is a conscious choice, and when burnout takes over, you are unconscious! No wonder cheating is so rampant, because burnout is!"[16]

By working with clients who have succumbed to infidelity, I have discovered that once they have cheated, they all deal with guilt. Thus, guilt is added to their stress and anxiety, which makes relationships suffer further and adds to the pain. If a leader who has committed adultery is married, there are issues to hash out to save or dissolve the marriage. If children are involved, there is another issue. If the affair occurred with a work associate or family friend, all hell on earth would come forth. Burnout has escalated to burned up!

Below are some recommendations for keeping infidelity off your resume.

- Spend quality time communicating with your partner.

---

[16] Weil, Bonnie Eaker, PhD. 2019. "Are You or Your Partner at Risk for Burnout Which Always Leads to Cheating?" DoctorBonnie.com

- Be honest and open with your partner about your current needs. Communicate.
- Have date nights and focus on your partner.
- Work to not be alone with a work associate you find yourself attracted to.
- Plan some 'guilt-free' leisure weekend time.
- Plan and make calendar time for vacations and getaways.
- Find a counselor who is a good fit for you and your spouse.

We have observed there are many ways to remove or prevent harmful weighty anchors of burnout. We must be proactive. Catch burnout before it strikes. For those of us who must look back at our burnout, let's do things differently than we did in the past. The past is there to be reflected upon and learned from so we can always get better at living our best lives. Every leader can improve, but it will not happen accidentally—it must be purpose-driven.

Fragmented Relationships

Every leader can attest that those who betray them are often the people they have given themselves to the most. This always hurts the deepest.

Andy Heartland, the leader of a nonprofit organization in the Dallas/Fort Worth, Texas, area will be the first to admit things can happen that may cause leadership to unravel at the seams. Andy shares his story:

> There were two amazing large families under my leadership. These were great people, and I was extremely proud of our association. These good people were hardworking and sacrificial

in giving of themselves and their resources to our organization. Both families had been in the organization for many years and had become influential within our community. These two families had a healthy intimate relationship with one another. Bad stuff happens. An awful situation developed that completely divided these individuals.

Two women, one from each family, had become best of friends. A tragic romance materialized and positioned these two women at odds with one another. One of these ladies had an inappropriate relationship that involved the other person's sibling. As one might imagine, word spread to both families, and the tension sailed to zenith proportions. My phone began ringing off the hook. In the midst of caring for a growing '501(c)(3),' I nor anyone else invited this tragedy. At this point in time, there were hundreds of individuals and families involved and serving in our institution. All of this caused a stir of emotions in many lives.

I did my best to lead both ladies and their families through a painful series of events and encouraged both families not to discuss matters related to the situation outside of their families. Yeah, right. I knew from past leadership tragedies that this was never going to happen. Each person in both families had best friends. Most of us tell our best friends intimate things. Word of the conflict spread just as the tension, confusion, and opinions did.

I had one-on-one meetings, two-on-two, three-on-three, then complete family meetings, and finally a joint meeting with most family members from both families present. I was the meeting moderator. Go ahead and tie my legs and feet to the back of a truck and pull me through a gravel pit. This would have given me more satisfaction. I reminded myself that this is what leaders do. Leaders guide people through pain and conflict to work toward the best resolution for everyone.

Without trying to play victim, I agonized over this more than I can explain with words. My heart was broken, and stress and anxiety took its toll on me. Why? I knew that I was in a 'catch-22' situation. 'Dang if you do, dang if you don't.' I was the bad guy either way. I felt extremely trapped. I wanted to take that cruise to 'somewhere' other than where I was at the time. Some members of both families expected me to tell several of the people from the other family to 'go take a hike' or 'make like a rock and roll' out of the place. I was doing everything that I knew to salvage everyone influenced by the disaster.

Relationships were fragmented, and there was no qualified resolution. Most of the family members from one side of the family peacefully left the organization. By that time there had been great relationship damage. They were in emotional trauma. The damage had spread beyond the two families. Andy picked up the pieces the best way he knew how and remained friends with everyone involved. Years later, both women apologized to Andy personally.

When tragic relational conflicts happen, it births a personal challenge to regain emotional strength to move forward. We achieve the momentum necessary to continue to lead, yet a mental scar makes its mark. This dramatic conflict takes more out of us than we realize. We feel betrayed by good people. They were hurting, and I have discovered that hurting people will hurt the people around them. This is a fact of life according to occurrences in my life journey, as well as in yours. When we are the leader of the organization, it is left to us to pick up the pieces and move forward. Even though we do not cause the problem, as leaders, some people blame us for the problem. Go figure.

The unsettling thing regarding the story I just shared is that so often in leadership, the leader has to take the lemons someone else created and make the lemonade for them. The commotion of the unfortunate relationship struggle was nothing the leader had caused. It was the leader's responsibility to attempt to resolve the issue and assist in bringing health and healing to two women and their families. In situations like that, it becomes an almost impossible task to handle.

In Summary

Realizing, admitting, and setting fear and pride aside while exercising appropriate self-care can help you heal from burnout, avoid burnout, and in general, be a better leader.

Both you and I have been handed scores of lemons to deal with and been tempted by negative thinking and the allure of easy escapes during our years of being a leader of others. Unfortunate things are going to happen and mistakes will be made, but it is the leader's responsibility to care for themselves, avoid loneliness and feeling trapped, and keep themselves from wrong so they can fulfill their leadership responsibilities.

We can learn from our experiences, our mistakes, and our pain, and from others who have traveled similar paths. When we keep ourselves aware of the anchors dropping and set alarms to recognize the warning signs, we will come much closer to preventing anchors settling to the bottom.

Being proactive gives us all the ability to prevent burnout from happening at all or from recurring. We must develop and implement boundaries in our lives so we can stay refreshed and make sure we never allow the mental anguish of burnout to invade and interrupt our lives again. Just like anything that lays an imprint in our minds, burnout can affect any one of us repeatedly. The addict suffering from any craving can relapse. I do not know you, but I know that you are capable of burning out again. How do I know that? Because you are a human being just as I am, and all of us have feet of clay.

Personally, since my burnout, I make a habit of staying aware of my weaknesses to not allow an anchor to drop. When I see the anchors or bad habits beginning to take hold of me, I try to stay cautious, so I don't get weighed down with them again. I have to stop and acknowledge what is happening. Learning from the anchors of bad coping mechanisms that have entangled you and other people are safeguards to manage a positive direction in our lives.

In the following chapter, we will discuss some things to keep all of us on the straight and narrow path of leading again and leading stronger. Building and fostering the right habits while avoiding the wrong ones is imperative to avoiding and recovering from burnout, so I am excited to share some of the habits for growth.

When people burn out, they sometimes think they are more than eager for something fresh and new. Generally, they have some ideas for something refreshing as a next step and, upon some phase of recovery, begin planning for this newness of life. The tendency for highly motivated leaders is to move *too* quickly, though. Slow down and keep dealing with each step in the process with the proper attention and time so you can overcome it.

Exercise:
Out with the Old

We have discussed the concept of not being weighed down by anchors that bad habits can bring. Ask yourself the following questions and then be transparent and vulnerable with your answers.

1. What are your bad habits?

   _____

2. What are your go-to methods for coping with anxiety and stress of leadership responsibilities?

   _____

3. What are your triggers that send you into each bad habit or temptation?

   _____

4. What habits would you like to replace those bad ones with?

   _____

5. What can you do proactively to keep yourself above reproach?

   _____

CHAPTER FOUR

Forgive the Pain Away

This is the pivotal point for every leader who has suffered the sting of burnout. I cannot reinforce this enough. Complete restoration will be determined by your ability to overcome the three-headed monster of resentment, guilt, and bitterness. Mark my words, every burned-out leader will internally battle these three enemies. If these emotions are not quickly identified and progressively overcome, recovery will be hindered, and for many, even impossible. Defeating these damaging feelings is critical for inner healing. This was true for me as I moved through my mental healing period and for the many other burned-out leaders I spoke with during and after my recovery.

Resentment

Resentment is a natural emotion felt when someone has brought pain, anger, or betrayal into the relationship. It is a painful emotion that erupts, leading to many mixed feelings. Resenting someone means not liking them right now. Because of painful feelings about them, you do not want to see them or communicate with them. The thought of their name can make your stomach queasy. This resentment continues to haunt you, and with time, it can get somewhat better, but the bad feelings will still be there.

The longer resentment goes unexamined and confessed, the deeper the emotion submerges into the memory bank of our pain. There is a part of a person's feelings that shut down, creating a loss of love, peace, joy, and compassion for the offender.

Often resentment leads to health issues. Yes, our bodies can be negatively affected by continued resentment. Unrelenting dislike for a person can lead to added anxiety, lack of sleep, harmful addictions, depression, high blood pressure, and many other enemies to the body.

Resentment will also poison a person's ability to forgive, which adds to the agony originally brought by the offense.

Guilt

Guilt is a normal response when a leader deeply regrets a decision related to their responsibility in a situation. 'What-ifs' and 'If I had only' can plague the mind.

> *What if I had made a different decision?*
> *What if I had handled that situation differently?*
> *If I had only given this employee one more chance…*
> *If only I would not have resigned…*

Sometimes a person is their own worst enemy, especially when they live with regret. Guilt sometimes combines other emotions, such as shame, anxiety, and humiliation. Feelings of guilt affect a person's self-worth and are common with mental disorders.

Guilt wastes emotional energy and life while fueling anxiety and, left unresolved so that it lingers on over time, can lead a person into depression. If one cannot release themselves from their guilt, they should seek professional help from a counselor, therapist, or a doctor.

Bitterness or Blame

Bitterness is the landing strip of resentment and guilt. It results from being emotionally hurt and thus having unresolved anger and/or guilt. Allowing these feelings to fester instead of working them out allows vicious emotions to build within. Bitterness creeps into an individual's mind, hardening their resolve to blame an external cause rather than focus forward on resolution. A bitter person can drown in sorrow and negativity, causing a drastic decrease in effectiveness, joy, and success in their personal endeavors and professional leadership role.

For a bitter person, just the thought of a person, hearing a person's name, or seeing the person considered the offender ignites painful and explosive emotions in the victim.

A bitter person:

- holds a grudge;
- blames the wrongdoer for their hurt;
- sulks;
- becomes prideful;
- gossips about their offender;
- is unrelenting in their hate;
- avoids happy people;
- becomes their own worst enemy;
- can be vicious and even violent against their offender;
- and will eventually extinguish their personhood without inner healing.

How are any of those feelings helping you achieve any of your goals?

We all know the answer to that question, do we not? A good leader must accept personal responsibility for not only their feelings and actions but the success of the company or organization. We must recognize the emotions of resentment, guilt, bitterness, and blame. We must be *pro*active and not *re*active. When we begin to sway in response to negative anchors that are wanting to drop, a mental alarm should sound to remind us that we are going off course. We must guard against negative emotions, let go of them, and stay the course that leads us to a successful passage.

Forgiveness

There is only one way to destroy the three internal enemies of resentment, guilt, and bitterness—*forgiveness*.

To forgive is to release the pain of resentment, guilt, and blame. Forgiveness is a process that is often much easier said than done. Do not take forgiveness lightly. The work to accomplish forgiving someone is well worth the effort. An unforgiving spirit has left many to self-destruction.

There have been times when I have known I needed to forgive someone but didn't want to. For some crazy reason, I wanted to keep the hurt, resentment, or bitterness to myself. There seemed to be an emotion inside of me that would rather keep the agony than give the offender the pleasure of knowing they have been forgiven. Most of us don't want to deal with forgiving people who have brought heartbreaking pain into our lives, because we mistakenly believe they will somehow benefit or be rewarded by being forgiven.

So, *why* should you forgive?

Often forgiveness is misunderstood to mean forgetting or excusing someone for the hurt and pain they caused. Forgiving an offender does not imply anyone is making up nor does it mean forgetting what happened and just picking up where you left off in your relationship. Forgiving is more for the offend*ed* than it is for the offend*er*. That's right, forgiveness is a gift for you, not the person who has made you feel hurt.

Forgiving is internally like having a change in feelings and attitude that allows us to overcome the impact of the offense. Emotions trick us and hold us back from living with inner peace, freedom, and growing in our personhood. It's about taking back control of your emotions so that all the negativity of carrying around resentment, guilt, and blame no longer rule you.

There are zero benefits to hoarding forgiveness but life-changing rewards in forgiving. The advantages are:

- Regaining personal power
- Obtaining inner peace
- Better blood pressure
- Lowering heart attack risks
- Getting more sleep
- Less anxiety, stress, regret, or depression
- Improved mental health
- Better all-around relationships
- Greater self-esteem
- Loving more
- Learning to trust honorable people

If you and I can forgive all the people in our lives who have offended or wounded us, that would mean we are *in control* of our emotions instead of *being controlled by* our emotions. Someone might label this type of behavior as growing up, maturing. If we do not resolve and come to terms with hurt, this emotion will drive our actions and create a negative person overall.

> "All illness is caused by not forgiving."
> —Native American belief [17]

Since most of us want to experience internal peace and rest, here is the way to begin that process. First, try to empathize with how your offender must be suffering to have caused you pain. We live in a selfish society, and sometimes selfishness rubs off on us. Get your mind off yourself and explore having some compassion for their pain. All of us need to get beyond ourselves. Too often, when the actions or words of someone emotionally wound us, we do not consider what is happening in the offender's life that brought them to adversarial actions.

Sometimes a person will overreact to someone in alignment with something personal that occurred in their life. Once, I took on a personal offense from one of my staff members. Someone dear to me made the wrong decision of impropriety that affected not only their lives but the lives of many others. My staff associate and their spouse became extremely vocal, hurling accusations and creating division against the person who had made the wrong decision. I took offense because they had been involved in a similar impropriety years earlier. I had loved and supported this couple as they wove through the turmoil of putting the pieces of their lives back together. To my remembrance, the staff member and their spouse had never shown any signs of sorrow, nor was there any apology made for their verbal abuse or complaints. Over time, I decided to forgive this couple because I recognized their reactions had surfaced because of the personal pain experienced by their own misdeed. Did I want to forgive

---

17 Ellerton, Roger. 2010. "Forgiveness." *Live Your Dreams Let Reality Catch Up: NLP and Common Sense for Coaches, Managers and You.*

them? Absolutely not. But I forgave them to attain personal peace with the situation.

Mistakes are going to happen—we are all human. Can you really be sure everything that offends you is intentional? Are you sure they weren't dealing with something that just prevented them from putting you first in that moment? And is it truly an offense to you that people sometimes have to put their own needs first in order to navigate the ups and downs of life?

Sometimes, empathy for others can defuse our offense and lend some compassion for others who are also hurting. Always, forgiveness is freeing for the one giving it.

But *who* should you forgive?

It is actually very common for leaders to take personal blame for all or part of any given situation, though one of the most dangerous things a leader can do is second-guess themselves.

> *It's my fault.*
>
> *If I had only listened.*
>
> *I made a decision too fast.*
>
> *I waited too long to make the decision.*
>
> *I could have prevented this.*

Internal reprimands are normal, and we can learn from them. As we take responsibility for our wrong actions, it is healthy to work on forgiving ourselves. It is the wholesome way to move forward. Until the leader forgives themselves, there will be no resolution. The emotional wound will remain open, become infected, and worsen.

It is imperative that we give ourselves grace enough to be human. Each one of us is capable of making terrible mistakes that we can never undo. We are not perfect. It's not whether or not we make mistakes, because we will no matter what, but it is what we do with these experiences that matters.

A senior leader I worked with experienced clinical burnout. She had always been a strict rule keeper while never trying to hold others to her personal requirements. As she began to emotionally heal, she had difficulty refraining from holding herself hostage with feelings of guilt and shame. After taking some time away from work, this leader returned to a new seat on the bus while continuing to fight her guilt for having left her previous job responsibilities in less than perfect shape and others having to take care of all that instead of her being able to handle it. It took this great leader a long time to reconcile that her previous burned-out frame of mind was unable to perform at a high level.

A person will remain in mental handcuffs, emotionally captive, until they forgive themselves because focusing on guilt and blame keeps us stuck, does not allow us to move forward. Neither you nor I can heal from burnout without forgiving ourselves. Invisible walls of defense or justification are subconsciously built slowly over time. Attempting to punish oneself by continuing to blame is narcissistic, which is unhealthy and self-defeating. Please understand that you do not deserve to hurt, and it is time to move beyond your pain and step into healing. If you do not forgive yourself, guilt and pain will destroy you.

When the web of self-punishment or self-hate has been woven tightly, it is often difficult to know how to forgive yourself. Burnout and self-judgment have the effect of a snowball rolling downhill. Until the snowball stops rolling, confusion and agonizing feelings continue to pack on. When I began trying to work through the mental gymnastics of forgiving people I felt added the fuel that ignited my burnout, I battled as much with forgiving myself for allowing things to affect me in the ways that they did as with forgiving others. In my confused state of mind, I had to remember something I had preached to others and put into practice innumerable times in the past. I needed to forgive, and it first required remembering how to forgive.

How Do I Forgive?

Embrace the truth that you cannot change the past. The lowest point of your life can be used for good. The very thing that you despise can become a platform for you to be whole again. Until the leader becomes vulnerable enough to themselves, it will be challenging to forgive other people. If you have not forgiven yourself of the things that lay like an open wound upon your mind, then the wall remains too high to climb to pardon those who have offended you. Destroy the barricade. Tear down the walls! To soften our hearts requires humility. We must uproot all the causes that led to burnout and forgive ourselves to enjoy the beginning of mental freedom.

I heard it said somewhere that hanging onto an unforgiving spirit is like a trapeze performer holding onto a trapeze. Consider your resentment represented by the trapeze bar you are holding onto. There's no net below, and you cannot swing to safety on your own. There needs to be a trapeze coming your way. That trapeze is called forgiveness. There is no other trapeze in sight for forgiving yourself other than the forgiveness trapeze. The only way to grab hold of the forgiveness trapeze is to let go of your trapeze of pain, anger, regret, resentment, and blame so you can grab hold of forgiveness with both hands.

Today is your healing choice—you must let go of the past. You know that you *cannot* change the past, but you *can* swing forward to healing and doing great things again. Allow me to simplify. Personal forgiveness is a requirement to rid yourself of the poison of an unforgiving spirit. Understand that these toxic emotions will only serve to destroy your life.

I became very ill during the summer of 2020 with a throat issue, the worst sore throat of my life. I had a virtual exam with my physician, and she scheduled a COVID-19 exam and prescribed medication. The COVID test proved negative, and the medications did not seem to work. Many days passed, and I went through the worst time of my life, unable to swallow and struggling to breathe. My throat felt as though it was lined with broken glass. I literally wanted to cry each time I tried to swallow. On Thursday of that week, a nurse from my clinic sent me to a local ER. I was quickly worked through the system because of all my symptoms. The ER physician examined me, and the nurses connected me with an IV and began administering morphine for the pain. I was sent for a CT scan to observe my throat. The results were that I had a throat abscess that needed to be lanced and removed.

The hospital ENT specialist could not attend to my situation for four hours, so I laid in the ER attempting to nap while I waited. When the doctor arrived, she observed my chart and my throat, prepared her instruments, and advised her nurse to give me more morphine. As I opened my mouth, she began to lance the abscess and compress it like someone trying to pop a pimple. I know this sounds gross, and it *was* gross. The attending nurse used a suction hose to remove the bile from my mouth, and I would, of course, use the tray to expel the remaining bile. The pain and the taste of the infection were almost unbearable, but I was willing to do whatever was necessary to gain relief.

After the physician went through this procedure four times, she said, "I think we removed all the infection."

I said, "You think? I'm willing to be certain if you have any doubt."

The doctor said, "Let's give it one more try."

The physician did just that. She made one final attempt to remove any remaining infection. After several minutes of allowing the pain from the procedure to subside, I began feeling immediate relief. The poison had been removed. I was released from the ER a couple of hours later after my vitals were better.

I never want to go through that type of procedure again, but I will gladly submit if I ever need it to remove a throat abscess. Why? Because even though it was extremely painful, it removed the poison from my body so that the pain would end.

Removing anger, resentment, hatred, and blame is painful, but the relief comes when these emotions have been extracted from our minds. I want to encourage you to go through the pain of past and recent memories to remove the poison of damaged emotions.

Below is a simple step-by-step process that can serve as a guideline to personal forgiveness.

- Acknowledge that you have tried to bury your feelings long enough.
- Admit that you harbor anger, self-resentment, hatred, and blame.
- Determine to forgive.
- Get away from distractions and write out in detail about your anger or blame.
- Now read your list of pain.
- Come to the reality that your unresolved feelings are like an anchor embedded in the muck and mire of deep ocean memories.
- Embrace that staying in this mindset will rot the inner you and inhibit future successes.
- Voice your mistakes or wrongs verbally.
- Leave the wrongs in the past but learn from them.

- Practice patience with yourself as you work through restoration step by step.
- This is a good time to get counseling from a therapist, counselor, or pastor.

Forgiving others is like forgiving yourself. You can use the same logic and same methods to forgive others. The principles are the same. It's the emotional baggage of resentment, guilt, and/or blame that holds us hostage, no matter who originally caused the pain.

The main thing that I battle when it comes to forgiving my offenders is simple. Often, I do not want to admit that I am bitter or holding a grudge against someone. Sometimes I know I must forgive people to keep growing as a person and a leader myself, but I don't want to forgive them. Sound familiar?

It is almost humorous if it were not so serious. Look at the process. First, I do not want to admit that I am harboring a hurt. Secondly, when I admit that I am hurt or resentful against someone, I do not want to release them from the offense. I do not 'feel like' forgiving them or forgiving them *yet*. I believe the reason for not forgiving the person moves to the third part in the process, which is that I do not want to go through the emotional pain of the memory and the struggle to forgive my offender.

Here is what I have to say to myself and any leader facing forgiving people who may not deserve to be forgiven. Find courage! One great aspect of your leadership talent has been your strength to endure many adverse situations. Use this determination to forgive your offender(s).

Forgive the people who have deeply hurt you for your and your family's sake. You must become whole again to be what your loved ones and friends deserve from you. To become whole, remove the poison of blame and resentment by forgiving your offender, and with what you've learned from the experience, establish boundaries to protect yourself from being a victim of bad behaviors again. Forgiving someone is like catching a fish, removing the hook, and tossing the fish back into the water to swim on its way.

This is how to forgive people who have hurt you:

- Admit that you are hurt, angry, or offended.
- Decide to forgive.
- Remember that you have been an offender.
- Consider the plight of the person who offended you.
- Speak to a person you trust and ask for their advice.
- Write out your feelings regarding your hurt.
- Contemplate personally speaking to or writing a letter to your offender. Expect nothing in return.
- If you are a person of faith, ask for help to forgive.
- Get counsel from a professional, such as a therapist, counselor, or life coach, if you cannot forgive.

I was working in mid-management at a well-established local business and achieving some success, moving up in the company. My direct supervisor and I did not see eye to eye on many issues, but he knew our business. I learned many things about the company, training, and managing people from him. One day I was training a new employee on my team and skipped some of the training processes on a particular project. It was the first time that I had done that. My supervisor observed my shortcut, pulled me aside, and quickly dragged me over the coals, figuratively speaking, for taking a shortcut in training a new employee. He was undoubtedly correct and I was wrong, but I took it personally and did not appreciate his harshness. I could not forgive my superior at first. I held it against him and could not enjoy being in his presence. Ultimately, I made a concentrated effort to forgive the man. I noticed I never made the same shortcut mistake in training people from that point forward. Even though I disagreed with how my manager reprimanded me, he led me to be better at training and managing those on my team.

It took forgiving that supervisor for how he dealt with my mistake for me to move forward and not feel stressed while at work and, ultimately, to get the most out of what needed to be learned from my mistake to begin with. By letting go of resentment and bitterness, we can find a way to forgive and move forward; we are better for the experience and no longer burdened by the three-headed monster that had been holding us back.

Exercise:
Forgive the Pain Away

Let's practice what we've learned so far from previous chapters. Be transparent with yourself and focus on the following:

1. Be honest with yourself and work through your burnout *realization*, *admitting* that you are burned out to yourself and to someone important in your life.
2. Have no *fear* and set aside your *pride*.
3. Next, reflect upon your *identity*.
   - Ask *who am I*? I am burned out and lost, mentally and physically fried.
   - Ask *what am I supposed to do*? My next steps are replenishing myself in both mind and body.
   - Ask *how am I to do it*? Map out your recovery plan using the tools and exercises provided.
4. Consider and accept the *heavy anchors* that led to your burnout. By accepting the *anchors*, you accept responsibility for them, even if you were victimized to some degree. Personal acceptance of everything will encourage you to let the anchor fall.
5. Forgive. Ask yourself if you have harbored resentment, guilt, bitterness, or blame, then:
   - Remember that forgiving someone is a gift for you, not the person who has made you hurt.
   - Forgive yourself of feelings that you let coworkers down.
   - Forgive those who you feel added to your pain.

CHAPTER FIVE
Recovering You—Healthy Habits

Someone said, "Laziness is the mother of all bad habits." I feel like the guy who said, "I don't have bad habits. I'm very good at all of them." Certainly, we can all agree that good habits are difficult to start and bad habits are difficult to stop. But being in more control of our habits is essential to happiness in all aspects of our lives, so definitely a critical component to avoiding or recovering from burnout in our professional lives. How can you lead others to have the good work habits their role requires if you don't lead by example?

We are all creatures of habit. It is especially easy for any of us to fall into bad habits, and many bad habits are not bad in the sense of being wrong. They are behaviors or lifestyles that become regular patterns but are not the best for us. As an example, nail-biting or procrastination can be considered bad habits. Good habits facilitate and nurture health and well-being and happiness, whether it's the good habits of personal care or good habits that encourage us to live satisfied and fulfilled lives. Good habits help us to be the best whole versions of ourselves.

Our lives are usually fast-paced, and it requires forethought and extra planning to do anything above the ordinary. We all get in our little groove, becoming a little too predictable sometimes. Most people will admit that most routine habits do not get us anywhere toward success. To be honest, a routine can make us as stale as a four-day-old biscuit.

When people become stuck in an unhealthy routine, they become mundane. Burnout usually finds the leader tightly wrapped up in unhealthy habits, in a cocoon-like mental health rut. The leader has been managing their mental health in the same fashion for so long that weariness and fatigue become painful contentment.

The burned-out leader should carefully process the components that led to burnout to define and then follow healthy habits purposely. Next, the journey will require a revisit of the anchors that drop too soon and cause burnout. Fallen anchors serve as the enemy of mental health and healing. Just so we do not stray from the right path, we will discuss steps for maintaining personal balance as post-workout habits. These things will help us preserve continuity on the road to recovery from burnout to mental wellness.

Take things slowly. Slower should be a *new habit*. Don't jump into anything quickly. Take your time while you confide in a close friend, doctor, therapist, coach, or counselor.

As the mentally wounded leader moves at a slower pace for a while, it is imperative to walk *purposely* through the steps provided in this manuscript. Don't cut corners. Some things will not apply as much as others. Work on the things that feel right for you, but in an honest way, fearlessly, without letting your pride interfere, and with the objective of getting the most out of every detail as possible.

It is vital to begin developing post-burnout habits at this point on the journey from burnout to restoration. New and healthy habits motivate the wounded to wholeness.

- Bad habits push leaders into the drudgery of burnout bondage.
- Good habits will gradually pull leaders out of the quagmire to rise above their confused state.

Don't Let Bad Habits Sink Your Ship

The *Titanic* is one of the most iconic tragedies in the modern world. Most people have read, seen movies, and watched or read documentaries on the subject. I have read that no one mistake sank that ship. Each mistake played a sad role in the *Titanic*'s demise. Other than the mistakes of Captain Edward Smith, there is one interesting mistake that explains the rapid speed at which the ship sank.

Titanic historian Tim Maltin said, "After the collision, the *Titanic* stopped, and people wondered what had happened. So, their natural reaction was to open the portholes and have a look. People fled to the lifeboats in panic mode and left the portholes open. As the *Titanic* passenger lodging area began to dip under the Atlantic, the open portholes meant that water flooded in at a much greater rate. In fact, twelve open portholes would have doubled the iceberg damage to *Titanic*—of course; there were hundreds of portholes in *Titanic*'s bow."[18]

Unfortunately, there is an uncanny parallel between the sinking of the *Titanic* and the sinking of many in leadership. Just like those unchecked portholes, unchecked health and undisciplined habits will sink the lives of leaders. Leaders need only

---
[18] 2023. Dailymail.com. "The 10 Mistakes that DOOMED the *Titanic*."
Quote by Tim Maltin. Published by Associated Newspapers, Ltd. Part of the *Daily Mail*, The Mail on Sunday and Metro Media Group.

leave just a few portholes open in their daily habits and quickly end up being consumed with the floodwaters of adversity.

I read a sign once that read something like this: "Ships do not sink because of the water they are on; they sink because the water gets in." That simple statement gives us the picture of so much truth. I have been on the water in small boats of ten feet or shorter, larger boats of thirty feet or more, and then my wife and I have been on a cruise ship of approximately 1,000 feet in length. Each time I have been in a boat or on a ship, I was keenly aware that no watercraft is unsinkable.

When a water vessel sinks, something has gone incredibly wrong. Some of the simple visible reasons ships can sink are strong winds, leaning at dangerous angles, and water forcing the ship lower or flooding the ship. Some catastrophes that sink ships are unavoidable even in perfect circumstances. But most sinkings could have been avoided by having good habits, like being more aware and responsive to weather alerts and not making mistakes in navigation. The same holds true for go*od leadership*. I have often heard that everything rises or falls owing to leadership. I do know that the buck stops with the leader. A leader leads. And to lead well, a leader should focus more on what needs to be accomplished than what not to do.

Over the twenty-five years of my leadership role, I wrestled with many health concerns, from anxiety, ulcers, a herniated disk with surgery and recovery, chronic stomach irritations, depression, discoid lupus, and the roller coaster of being overweight. Three times I went on diets and lost fifty pounds. After working feverously to lose weight, I ate like a pro and gained all the weight back in twelve months. Last but not least, I fought physical and psychological burnout.

I made attempts to get proper exercise during my twenties and thirties, but my inconsistency with the gym brought little help. I was forced to take things seriously in my midthirties when I herniated a disk in my lower back. I partially recovered with a few months of physical therapy but was forced to have surgery. The injury required a laminectomy, and in six months, I herniated a disk once more while playing basketball with some friends. Back to therapy I went.

Over the next twelve years, I herniated a back disk at least six times. I had a great therapist who taught me awesome self-healing techniques, and I have been able to apply these exercises to keep myself off the operating table for many years.

Good habits bring a good reward. When I was in my early forties, I decided I wanted to learn how to defend myself, get in good physical condition, and learn some martial arts. My wife, daughter, and youngest son enrolled in a kung fu class. We worked hard, and all four of us earned our white sashes together. My son and I continued another year or so and earned the blue sash, which is about halfway to black. I stayed with kung fu a couple more years and worked up to the purple sash. The next step is the black sash. I was close to achieving the black when our martial arts school closed.

During the four years spent going to kung fu, usually twice per week, many fruitful benefits poured into my life. My health improved, I was able to keep my weight under control, and I enjoyed a focused frame of mind to be successful in my work. On top of these wins, I learned how to defend myself and enjoyed sparring with classmates. I did enroll in one mixed martial arts tournament. I participated in one three-minute match, and yes, of course, I outscored my opponent. I must mention that he was ten years younger than I. Yes, I thought that I was a bad-a. Good and healthy habits produce good and healthy results.

I was around fifty years of age when I suffered burnout. I had stopped working out, was fifty pounds overweight once more, and because of high work demands and people issues, I was a sinking ship.

Good Habits Keep Your Ship Afloat

Thirteen years ago, my employer gave me a day off from work and paid thousands of dollars for me to get a complete physical from head to toe, blood tests, stress tests, EKG, and an echocardiogram. The tests revealed some disturbing information regarding my health. I immediately changed my diet and began exercise and weight training in a local gym. I lost fifty pounds (there I went again) and built muscle. To this day, I have maintained a healthy weight and have more visible muscle than I have ever had. I work out hard at the gym at least three to four days per week. My wife and I attempt to eat healthy most (*ha ha*) of the time; come on, give me a break.

What is the fruit of good habits? Well, fruit is the product of something that has grown and become productive. By the way, your life bears fruit, either good or bad. The fruit of good habits is the result of doing good and productive things. The fruit that we bear is our reputation and the outcome or results of applying ourselves to the practice of planning our day, setting simple goals, and purposely showing gratitude and respect to those at work. When a person who has experienced burnout begins to discipline their life with good and wholesome daily habits, they will become healthy in their thinking, which will lead to fulfillment in life again.

Positive and Healthy Habits for Smooth Sailing

Observe your Life Patterns – Addictive Tendencies, Personal Inventory, Isolation—Beware! When red flags appear, take note to correct the areas that push you toward a downward path. This is a bold and courageous first step on the road to facing and coping with burnout. This allows the wounded leader to make a genuine personal assessment of where they are in life.

Get to Know Your Body—Listen to your body! You read it correctly. Learn to listen to what your body is telling you and then act on meeting those needs. If your body says, "I'm hungry," then eat. Stop and replenish yourself when your body says, "I'm weary." Your body will usually tell you when you are ill. Pay attention and take the necessary steps to take care of your health. Don't postpone self-care to avoid appearing weak or less than a superhero. Be human and take great care of your human body. Your longevity greatly depends on how well you get to know your body and respond to its needs.

Remember From Whence You've Come—None of us arrive where we presently are overnight. Think of all the *good people* who have invested themselves in you over time. Consider the many who have followed your leadership, partnering with you to accomplish great things. Remember them all and continue in gratitude *for* them and *to* them.

Slow Down—We have brought attention to slowing down, but the slower pace is critical when a person is emotionally and physically rebuilding. A person's heavy schedule will cross paths with weariness and burnout. Now is a time to plan on doing life differently, positively. Most leaders are self-motivated and self-starters. Doctors suggest that we slow down to recalibrate our momentum for a healthier life.

Get to Bed Early and Get up Early—These two practices can do wonders for anxiety and stress. The way we begin our day and how we close out the day does have much to do with our mental health. Don't take life for granted. Respect yourself by not wearing yourself out. Coming back from burnout requires good health and energy. Instead of trying to impress people, slow down and do what is right for you.

Journal Your Way—Just write what is on your mind and highlight sentences that speak to you for future review. Upon rising, then meditate, write, pray, think, and reflect. Journaling will help improve your mood, empower you to self-check, and reduce symptoms of anxiety or depression. In a chapter to come, I will provide details for a successful journaling journey.

Accept Your Current Place in Life—I once heard, "If 'ifs and buts' were candy and nuts, we would all have a merry Christmas." Post-burnout is a difficult place for anyone to be. Accept your current place in life by not reliving painful past situations. Accept your identity and the building process of emotional and mental wellness. Accept that your leadership may have changed and encourage yourself that good days are still to come.

Get Good Accountability—Accountability is crucial for you and me to become the best we can be. Be in a hurry to bring the right person into your life. We will explore accountability thoroughly in chapter six.

Improve Your Diet and Exercise—All right, I am not a physician, but I know firsthand how diet affects a person's feelings. Proper diet greatly affects the health of a person and their happiness. We all have read about proper exercise and diet giving quality of life and helping to delay health issues. Remember, your health is more important than your work.

Check Points to Prevent Sliding Back—Every successful leader I have known has overcome obstacles and developed the discipline to be responsible for a company or organization. Now it's time to use your management skills to manage yourself and develop checkpoints to progress in greatness again and again without backsliding.

Mindfulness—Mindfulness may be easily described as *'being or staying in the moment.'* To place yourself in the moment, all five senses—sight, sound, smell, taste, and touch—should be engaged. Mindfulness helps bring focus and relaxation. It is practiced by taking in all five senses one at a time. This simple procedure may be illustrated by making coffee, tea, or orange juice in the morning. A person begins by sitting down and pouring the drink into the container. While looking at the cup or glass and the color of the liquid, start calmly smelling the liquid. Usually, a person will like the taste and how their favorite beverage will smell. Take in all the smells slowly, then feel the warmth or chill of the glass or cup. Enjoy your drink and take time to taste the substance. This practice has reduced stress, anxiety, and depression in many clients exposed to Mindfulness-Based Therapy (MBT).

Chill More, Enjoy More Play—Take time to enjoy the hobby of your choice. Perhaps find a new hobby. This should be an activity that refreshes you. Put down the phone, move away from the computer, and *unwind*. In the busyness of your world, few people realize that 'chilling out' or relaxing will boost a person's health and make one's work performance more productive. Good chemicals and growth hormones rise to new levels. Have some good belly laughs with a loved one or a friend.

Create Fun Habits—Release the happy chemicals. Happy hormones mean a happy person. In the medical field, they call them 'neurotransmitters.' There are also good hormones or chemicals produced by glands in the body and then released into our bloodstream. These hormones activate your moods and health.

- *Serotonin* is a feel-good hormone that is mainly produced by the gut.

- *Oxytocin* is called the 'cuddle or feel-good hormone.' This hormone secretes in response to certain types of eye contact, touch, and times of stress.

- *Dopamine* is the hormone that brings happiness while involved in a wide range of activities.

- *Endorphins* are the runner's hormones that function as pain signalers. Boost endorphins with cardio fitness. [19]

---

19 McCallum, Katie. 2021. "Brain Chemistry & Your Mood: 4 Hormones That Promote Happiness." Houston Methodist.

Fun and enjoyment are supposed to be a normal part of life, as the very design of our bodies indicates. Make time for fun and relaxation in your habits to enjoy a well-balanced lifestyle that in turn helps you avoid or recover from burnout.

Ideas for Adding Fun and Enjoyment to Your Life

- Laugh at yourself; it's healthy.
- Go walking; exercise at least three times per week.
- Do something that is fun to you, guilt-free.
- Exercise.
- Play golf, hunt, or go fishing.
- Take martial arts or don't.
- See a movie.
- Add popcorn and a dill pickle to that movie.
- Read a book or two.
- Talk to an old friend and get some laughs.
- Listen to music that relaxes you or music that you enjoy singing along with (private karaoke, very private—just teasing).
- Work on a puzzle.
- Learn something new each day.
- Do a crossword puzzle; it's good for the mind.
- Play a table game. It's a lost art; my wife always beats me, and we don't play much.
- Eat a banana split. Share it with your significant other or tell them to get their own.
- Meditation—get quiet, focus, and reflect.
- Practice mindfulness techniques.

- Take slow deep breaths and stretch.
- Repeat as often as you wish or need to.
- One of my favorites is to eat a meal with loved ones and friends.

The following chapter will discuss a powerful life-giving tool to help keep us on track with our habits. I know one thing for certain. Both you and I need accountability to help keep us focused on being the best we can be. You are an amazing person to have stayed on this journey with me. Thank you, and rest assured you will be amazed at your personal growth and happiness.

Exercise:
In With the New

Being a leader requires us to lead the pack with expertise and positivity every day. This is why it is so important to make productive healthy habits foundational to our agenda. Purposely commit to the new healthy habits to reign supreme as the best leader you can be.

What are some healthy habits leaders should practice daily?

- Read daily good articles and books (Leaders are readers).
- Plan your day the day before.
- Be loving, caring, and decisive.
- Live with integrity.
- Be open, honest, and vulnerable.
- Lead by being a good example.
- Serve people, place them before yourself.
- Have daily goals, to-do lists.
- Write things down; don't rely on memory.
- Eat healthily and exercise.
- Have a good attitude.
- Keep focus and practice mindfulness.
- Say thank you, it was my fault, and I am sorry.

Chapter Six

*Recovering You—
Keeping Account of Your Ability*

I was with a good friend who was also my mentor on the way to have lunch one day, and since both of us were leaders in our separate organizations, we were sharing stories. It seemed out of nowhere that my friend said to me, "Don, you don't believe in that accountability crap, do you?"

Taken aback, I had to think about the best way to reply without being offensive. I responded by saying something like, "I believe certain types of accountabilities can be healthy."

What is accountability? Accountability means that a person is responsible for the task they have been given. An employer told me, "People don't do what you expect, they do what you inspect." Every leader as well as every individual who has been given a responsibility is accountable for fulfilling that responsibility.

For example, if you are the senior sales manager of a major automobile distributor and your sales benchmark is 100 cars per month, but you only sell seventy-five, you will be accountable to your superior for missing your sales target by twenty-five cars.

If you are the parent responsible for taking your child to their baseball game and having them there by 9:00 a.m. on Saturday and you arrive at the ballpark at 9:15 a.m., your tardiness has consequences because you did not fully or properly fulfill your responsibility. You have placed embarrassment on your child and negatively affected his or her ball team because you were late.

We must accept personal accountability for every area of our lives, our job, our department, our projects, leading meetings, motivation of our work team, our family, our personal dreams, and our goals. There is no room to discount our failure nor make excuses when we fall short of achieving our tasks.

If we're not taking responsibility for our actions or lack of actions, who will? If we allow ourselves to lay blame rather than take responsibility, how will anything get done? How can we achieve a healthy work-life balance of good habits without taking responsibility?

Accountability and leadership, in many ways, have been given a bad rap. Many organizations have set leadership up with a destructive structure for the leader and the organization. That is *bad* accountability. Having too many hoops to jump through inhibits a leader's freedom to lead and can cause time wasters, make projects unnecessarily too long, breed unwanted tension among teams, and overall morale can suffer.[20] On the other hand, leaders with no accountability may create and/or nurture destructive patterns, like a lack of trust, unclear priorities, ineffective execution, low morale, and even high turnover of employees. Let me make this practical. A boss should explain perimeters, perhaps with some dos and don'ts, but working for a micromanager is equally challenging. There has to be a balance of enough direction and support, freedom and accountability,

---

20 Maloyan, Joseph. 2023. "4 Ways to Deal with Bosses Who Make Us Jump Through Hoops." Young Hero Engineer.

for the leader to lead their people in delivering the results the company wants.

Global research led by Vince Molinaro discovered that 72 percent of business leaders and human resource professionals all concur that to have business success, it is vital to have accountability and that accountability in leadership at the top level sets the tone for all of the leadership levels in an organization.[21]

> *Accountability basically means accepting accountability for oneself and the goals and objectives of the organization and leading the team to have the same focus.*

Just like most leadership principles, accountability needs to be anchored in the foundation of who we are as a person, in our personal lives, to produce positive results. It is up to each of us to develop balance in our personal lives, and if we can do that, it will become more natural to construct balance in our leadership roles as well.

Accountability begins for all of us in our personal lives, one-on-one with ourselves. Being accountable to ourselves establishes our purpose and gives us a reason for being and doing. I can become my own worst enemy if I get off track in life, and this tends to be the case for many people. There are so many voices and so many things speaking to us. Staying on track in our personal life and goals can be a challenge, but one well worth being aware of and hitting head on. I know that if my personal life is suffering from fatigue, anxiety, or disappointment, it will be a bigger challenge to be strong in leading my organization. My mental sharpness to communicate vision and focus will be foggy if I am foggy. Therefore, I must reiterate the need for personal clarity and accountability as a foundation for everything else in life.

---

21 2021. "Accountability in Leadership." Betterworks.com.

I found J. D. Meier's book *Getting Results the Agile Way* incredibly helpful for learning new and better ways to ensure I can maintain clarity and get results more consistently. Consider grabbing a copy to add to your toolbox as it offers a simple systematic approach to better short and long-term results in all areas of your life. My key takeaways as they relate to recovering from or preventing burnout were: Take some time to actually get away from the waves of life that keep rocking your boat. To do that we must intentionally remove the distractions of the cell phone, computer, and television to disconnect from the chatter that keeps splashing unnecessary distortion into our minds. Get alone and give yourself time to dream, remember your life purpose, and become a visionary, perhaps like you have been in the past. The freshness and newness of mental clarity can remind us that we are accountable for the productivity of our lives. And this accountability will feel like a good thing rather than a burden.

We must be aware and conscious that we have to work on ourselves to stay sharp and productive and hold ourselves accountable for doing so consistently, or the distractions and derailing bad habits will too easily be able to interfere. It is work, nothing short of hard work, but the results will be pleasurable and worth it.

Ask yourself, "Am I willing to be accountable?" If you are willing and ready to make yourself accountable to yourself and others, you should continue working on your mental healing. Understand that it is okay not to be ready. You have suffered the trauma of brokenness, and proper healing must occur. It is difficult to place a time frame on that. But you do need to be ready to hold yourself accountable to be successful with this step in the process of avoiding or recovering from burnout.

You have to be open and honest with yourself. I believe we must stand back and ask ourselves, "What does accountability look like in my life?" It will look different for you than for one of our peers or for me because we are all unique individuals with different temperaments.

Give yourself some attention in this area. Sit down with a pen and paper or find a whiteboard and markers and intentionally list some things you need to focus on. Be open and honest with yourself. Find a way to refocus by directing your attention to get a clear picture of what you wish to accomplish. List out what accountability looks like for you. Answer the question, "To whom am I accountable, and what are my true desires?" Be sure to keep it simple and clear out external and internal distractions. Do not chase every idea that runs by you. Stay clear on what you need and feel. Know your priorities!

Accountability Is Not that Difficult, Don't Make It Hard

Really, what we want to accomplish on a personal level is self-awareness. We desire to understand our unique patterns. We want to learn our usual mindset. More on mindset will be shared in the next chapter.

Bring others into your life for accountability. Over the years, I have had various groups of accountability partners. It is wise to have the same gender as you are on these teams. Some of the discussion subjects make it more appropriate to have same-sex members or those you are not physically attracted to.

Accountability team members are there for one another, supporting one another. This means that often hard questions need to be asked of each other. Perhaps you have had a bad experience with this type of group, but that does not mean all groups of this nature will lead to a sour taste in your mouth. Keep trying until you get it right. When you do get it right, it is extremely rewarding and encouraging. It is amazing to watch team members grow in their personal lives just as you grow in your own.

Here is just one example of how to structure your accountability group or team:

- Decide who is the right fit for your group—yeah, buddy, handpick your group.
- Usually, 3-5 people is the right number of people.
- Clearly define the purpose of this team.
- Decide together the right venue, times, and frequency to meet.
- Set a time frame for the group to meet; three, six, or twelve months.
- Discuss how deep the group will grow—how much information you will share.
- What is said in the group must stay in the group—confidentiality is imperative.

We have only one life on this planet, and it is short at best. It behooves you and me to find ways to make this life the best and the most profitable that it can be. Personal accountability is part of the healthy process for all of us. Let us keep moving.

Dead people don't wish they had worked more hours. We all know it's true that dead people don't wish they had stayed at the office or the shop longer each day. We don't know this for certain because there is no way to ask them, but it's easy to assume that we can count on that being the truth.

So many of us leaders are tempted to be the first person at work and the last person to leave, the one working weekends, but why? We want to be the best on the job and feel responsible for the success of the corporation. But is that way of life balanced or all-consuming?

There have been many great quotes about too much work. You and I may not agree with all of them, but many of them are thought-provoking. I want to share a few:

> *Balance in work is not better time management but better boundary management. Balance means making choices and enjoying those choices.*
> — Betsy Jacobson

> *A woman who lives with the stress of an overwhelmed schedule will often ache with the sadness of an underwhelmed soul.*
> — Lysa Terkeurst

> *Your energy is currency. Spend it well.*
> — Adrienne Bosh[22]

While not every person has a significant other, children, or pets demanding they arrive at home daily at a certain time, it is vital to balance work life and personal life for yourself anyway. You may be thinking, "Oh, really, Captain Obvious? Who doesn't know that?" Knowing that we should balance our work and personal lives and doing something about it are often two separate things. Holding yourself accountable for keeping good habits is the key.

Reasons to go home and not work so much even if you're single:

- Your physical health
- Your mental health
- Too much work prevents good sleep and rest

---

22 Bhuyan, Nizamul. 2021. "40 Best Too Much Work Quotes to Cope Stress and Burnout." Vantage Fit.

- Creating good habits, not bad habits
- Overworking can cause you to make more mistakes
- Too much work can cause heart problems
- When you work too much, it ultimate damages your creativity

When the company demands you to work overtime too much, there may need to be a come-to-Jesus meeting. It may take guts to do this—excuse me, I intended to say intestinal fortitude. Hopefully, you can intelligently and calmly confront the supervisor to let them know your life demands some lifestyle changes. Let them know you need their help. You want to give your all to the business and can be a better employee when you take care of yourself. And be willing to choose a different job or profession if that will be the only way to meet your needs. Just use common sense and pay attention to the way you feel.

In addition to those reasons for self-care, this next section is for those with a significant other and/or children.

Let's be transparent. It should take no convincing that you need to be home. Yes, you need to be home as much as humanly possible. Your partner or significant other needs you. Your children need you. The dynamic formative years of a child are between one day old and eight years old. And no one wants to miss out on the joys of watching their children grow up through any phase of their youth. There is no substitute for a mother or dad spending time with their family. These words are not written to make anyone feel guilty. We must face the reality that the kids are only young once. Most people I know juggle the challenges of work, being a good employee, and going home as soon as possible each day.

Just as a leader works hard to organize and plan things for team building at work, efforts should be made to build your team at home, the family. Parents pour into each other's life, and together you pour your love, guidance, wisdom, common sense, and knowledge into your children's lives. It is a lifelong process. A parent never stops being a parent. Children grow up, but a parent's love and support never stops. If you work with your partner in building the family team, the dream works best with teamwork. Be consistent in your parenting, not letting work frustrations or weariness override how you would normally parent or prevent you from being present at all.

Significant other relationships also demand personal time. For the relationship to grow and provide both partners with what they need from it, one-on-one time is essential. Because of the busy lifestyles of the twenty-first century, all of us must work on spending intentional time with our loved ones.

Supporting your partner is a decision. What I will state next rubs many people the wrong way in our culture, so buckle your seatbelt. The goal of one spouse must be to put the other first. Yes, put them first and place yourself second. True relationships that thrive and survive do so because each person in the relationship loves the other person greater than they love themselves. If both partners are thinking of the other first, they are both lovingly being taken care of. When you live your life this way, there will be fewer problems within the relationship dynamics because you are not working from selfishness that doesn't consider the other person's needs and desires.

We all realize that since none of us are perfect, we will mess up and mess up royally. Couples share in accountability in every area of doing life together. There are three major contributors to marital relationship problems:
- Communication
- Trust
- Finances

I want to talk about the first two contributors to the couple's struggles: communication and trust.

My wife and I have been married for almost a lifetime, and communication is as vital to us getting along as it was the first year we were married. Most of us know what happens when we assume something. I will not indulge in assume's wordplay, but I think you get the picture. "I assumed you were picking the kids up today." Or, "I assumed you were feeding the dogs early tonight since we were going to the concert." Generally, it's a lack of communication in the everyday little details that causes tension and frustration within our relationships.

Communication struggles can be reduced by awareness and a desire to be responsive and accountable to your mate. Here are some guidelines that can strengthen couples' communications:

- Talk it out—make time to spend time with one another.
- Listen well—not just hearing what the other person said but listening to what they feel and need.
- Keep them in the bus—don't throw the other person under the bus.
- Use encouraging statements, which never begin with, "You never…" or "You always…"
- Think before speaking—don't make it a blame game.
- Decide to understand your mate's point of view rather than focusing on wanting your point to win the discussion.
- Talk about the present and future, but be careful not to bring up the painful past.

The "10-Minute Rule" is a phrase coined by Dr. Terri Orbuch, who studied 400 couples over thirty years and discovered that happy marriages spend at least ten minutes per day talking about meaningful things. In reality, the average couple spends less than four minutes a day in a meaningful conversation.[23] As you map out your good habits, this is a small change that would be so easy to make, to just add those six more minutes.

Trust is the foundation of strong relationships, especially marriage. Trusting one another is giving honor to one another. When one partner has lost trust in the other, a slick slope leads to trust destruction. Trust can be rebuilt, but it will take a long time for it to be as deep or forgiving as it once was. There are many well-known causes of lack of trust in marriages: lying, insecurity, emotional or physical affairs, and broken promises, to mention only a few.

Warren Buffett said, "It takes twenty years to build a reputation and five minutes to ruin it."

George MacDonald stated, "To be trusted is a greater compliment than to be loved."

And Bob Vanourek, author of *Triple Crown Leadership*, noted, "Trust is when someone is vulnerable and not taken advantage of."[24]

It benefits all of us to positively practice the things that build or rebuild trust with one another. Here are some ways we can accomplish strengthening trust:

- Be open and vulnerable with one another.
- Think the best so you always give your partner the benefit of the doubt.
- Always be truthful even if it hurts. It will hurt worse if you lie and get caught, and eventually, you will get caught.
- Always respect the other person.

---

23 Smalley, Dr. Greg and Erin. 2020. *Reconnected: Moving from Roommates to Soulmates in Marriage*; Study Guide. Focus on the Family.
24 Daskal, Lolly. 2015. "30 Quotes on Trust That Will Make You Think." *Inc.*

- Work together for the good. Manipulation must not be part of your habits.
- Say "I am sorry and forgive me" as necessary.
- Release anger without yelling.
- Know the details and do not accuse.
- Share your fears and doubts and ask for the help and grace of the other.
- Agree to disagree and commit to unity no matter what.

One of the keys in a relationship is to rekindle the rapport by being intentional. Julie Holmquist, a content provider for the Focus on the Family marriage team, said:

> When my husband, Jeff, and I were juggling life with four teenagers, two jobs, and all the regular maintenance of living, it was easy to ignore our marriage relationship. There were times when I asked myself, *Who is this guy?* Sure, he gets the oil changed in the cars, picks up the kids from extracurricular activities, and makes waffles on weekends. But what happened to *us*?
>
> Decades of marriage and full family life can extinguish the fire that helps couples first connect and become close. But our relationship with God offers a template for rekindling a relationship. We don't have to be the victims of time and busyness. If we're intentional in a few ways, we can reconnect with our spouse instead of drifting apart.[25]

---

25 Holmquist, Julie. "How to Rekindle a Relationship with Your Spouse." 2022. Focus on the Family. Excerpted with permission. Originally published on FocusOnTheFamily.com.

In a lifelong relationship, a couple may need the intervention of a professional, such as a pastor, counselor, therapist, or doctor. Do not be afraid to reach out. After all, your commitment to each other is worth the risk, expense, and vulnerability.

Family Time—Make it Educational and Fun

Finding the balance between work and family requires determination and planning. All of us have experienced being so tired that we are zonked when we have time set aside to spend with family. Your good habits, including self-care routines, will make changing that easier, more achievable, but you can also plan accordingly to still be able to spend that time even when you're overtired.

Remember that not all family time should be a party. Sometimes, simple and fun events for the whole family will be better for you and your family. Yes, we are accountable to our families, and we are responsible for giving them our best.

- Make family time a priority—Make setting aside special days/times a weekly habit that everyone will look forward to.

- Work together on chores around the house—Even the little ones can learn to participate in chores on their level. They will not get it right, but it will be productive as they get older and practice more. Do some fun things, like games, playing with animals, or having a picnic in the backyard. Breaking the chores up between the fun stuff will be beneficial for the whole family.

- Decide together on a joint project or a trip to a local site: Mowing the yard, raking leaves, building a playhouse, building a birdhouse, or building a picnic table. You could visit an interesting museum, a fair, or an amusement park; go fishing; or work together at a food pantry.

There are many ways to have fun and spend quality time together with the family while also learning practical things and educating your family. It will be challenging to develop ideas that will please everyone, given the age variations within a family unit, but you can be creative to distinguish ways to include everyone. As the kids get older, they often want to include one of their close friends to participate in some family events. There is a time and a place for the kids to invite a friend, and there are times it needs to be only family. Have fun as you work on that one.

As the family grows, you may want to decide together on family vacations. Over the years, my family has made Disney World and Universal Studio in Orlando, Florida, a favorite destination. Even while I was writing of this book, our adult children and grandchildren were looking forward to large family retreats to such places.

There are many ways to spend family time together and make it special. As we prioritize our family, we begin making memories of a lifetime. The adult children will even want their children to experience some fun places they enjoyed as a child.

One thing is for certain, children spell love as *time*. The time together does not have to be large chunks of time. Sometimes time spent will be thirty minutes or one- or two-hour segments. Consistency and quality are the important elements. You are bonding together, and that is the important thing. You need family time as much as your other family members need it, and accountability to family time becomes a blessing to everyone in the family.

Since getting out in public and dealing with all types of people is a big part of life, we should learn to be pros with what I will call *relationship habits*. Below is a checklist of ideas and good relationship habits that we will be wise to practice.

Do Unto Others

Do unto others as you want them to do unto you. Yes, I'm mentioning this again because it is an important part of being authentically you and holding yourself accountable. That statement is called the Golden Rule for a reason. It is other-centered, not self-centered. Put yourself in the other person's shoes before speaking/acting, asking yourself if you were in their same situation, possibly dealing with things that might derail you, as you may well be right now, what would you need? There is no shortage of ways to *do unto others*, so I will list enough to get you started:

- Treat others with generosity.
- Show appreciation for the generosity of others.
- Give respect.
- Instead of judging someone, build them up.
- Listen instead of talking too much.
- Give the benefit of the doubt.
- Encourage and compliment people when you get the opportunity.
- Always remember that other person's life is as valuable as your life is to you.
- Value the other person's opinion.
- Be truthful.
- Avoid gossip.
- Revere people's privacy.

Just like a mirror, all the ways we treat others will reflect on us, the good and the bad. When you and I treat people the way we want to be treated, we will find peace and fulfillment. Not too long ago, I left a large, well-known store and was headed to my car. As I began to open my car door, I observed a small lady of the senior citizen variety wrestling with a large plastic package of bottled water. She had it in her arms and was struggling to lift it high enough to place it in the back seat of her truck. I carefully approached her vehicle and asked if I could be of assistance, and in between labored breaths she said, "Yes, please!" I took the package from her and placed the bottles of water where she was attempting to place it. She smiled and thanked me, and as I proceeded to get into my car, I must admit that I felt very good about my Boy Scout behavior of helping that lady. It was a simple act, yet I felt a sense of fulfillment by helping her the way I would want someone to help me.

Don't Take Yourself Too Seriously

One good way to adjust an overinflated sense of pride is to accept our humanity, frailty, and depravity. Come on now...we are all messed up. I am a public speaker, and I have mentioned on many occasions, "We all need counseling." Humility tells us this is true at some point in life. The person who tries to convince themselves they have it all together is struggling with insecurity.

Butch D. Ray, the CEO of a midsize company, says, "Because of my insecurities, I do not always find it simple not to take myself too seriously. I do not like for others to see me fail at something. Having thick skin is a trait that leaders should embrace, but I have battled with it my entire life. When I get my feelings hurt, I attempt to remind myself that I am taking myself too seriously quickly."

The question then is, how can I learn and practice not taking myself too seriously?

1. Learn to laugh at yourself.

   This is sometimes difficult for me. If I am doing a public speech and do something such as give the date of a known world event incorrectly, someone will always straighten me out on it. That is a small thing. This can upset me, not because I was corrected by someone, but rather because I strive hard to be accurate and don't like failing. Being upset is not aimed at the person who corrected me but with myself. I must practice *laughing at myself*. If you slip and fall, it is all right to pick yourself up and dust yourself off and laugh about it unless you were injured by the fall. The key is not to take yourself so seriously that it affects your life or the life of others negatively.

2. Accept your imperfections.

   All of us have imperfections, whether there is something about us that is physically different, a speech impediment, or other blemishes. I am not suggesting that you mention the flaw or laugh at yourself. What I am suggesting is that you do not allow that imperfection to hold you back from being who you are meant to be. A healthy way to handle our imperfections is to use our weaknesses to be a strength. We can do this by embracing our discomforts and facing our fears. Discomforts could be something such as disliking confrontation. Use that weakness and be gentle and bold when confrontations come. Face your fear with your inherent dignity and strength that is within. There is only one of you, the good, the bad, and the ugly (tongue in cheek). Be the best you that you can be. Love yourself and how you are made to positively affect other people's lives.

3. When you mess up, relax.

   My daughter and son-in-law have a great family pet named Skye. When this family dog gets too active and overly excited, they look at her and say, "Skye, relax." They say it slowly, like reeellaaaxx. Skye will lie down and relax. In the same way, you and I need to take a chill pill and relax when we mess something up. Give it a few moments. Allow your emotions that spiked because of the mess up to settle down. Then you can move forward positively.

4. Wanting reassurance can be good, but limit your need for it.

   It is wholesome to get reassurance for many things in our lives. While we gain information and creativity from the input of others, we should limit how much we need, how much we depend on that feedback. Get enough and skim the cream off the top of the advice. Take the added wisdom or the inspiration and apply it to what you want. The limiting aspect comes from the tendency we can have to be a people pleaser. Be who you are meant to be. The counsel that someone gives you is only to enhance what you think is best or to be a help in qualifying the direction you are proceeding. Be careful not to base your final decision upon pleasing someone else. Just do the right thing for yourself.

5. Enjoy your life journey.

   Life is too short to live in the past and stay stuck in the present. Keep your energy up by taking care of yourself, reading positive material, and focusing on what is right for you. Place your focus on the bigger good that is just beyond you and be sure to reward yourself along the journey. Do what is necessary to find inspiration that keeps you wanting to get up another day to make your life count.

Keeping account of your public life will always be important. It should not become a struggle and if it does, work on recalibrating your vision and goals. Love yourself and love other people. Learn from personal mistakes and learn from the mistakes of others. Everything we have discussed in this chapter can be controlled with having the right focus and mindset. This is going to be enlightening and fun.

Exercise:
Keeping Account of Your Abilities

Accountability begins in our personal lives. Ask yourself the following questions and answer them with intention and purpose.

1. Do you have some accountability in place with any of these?
   __ A person close to you
   __ A group of three to five people
   __ A counselor, therapist, or coach

2. What is the purpose of your accountability person or team?
   __ To check up on your health (physical and mental well-being)
   __ To help you keep focus on your life, job, and family
   __ To discuss real issues and allow you to receive feedback

3. Do you set aside time to be vulnerable with a spouse, significant other, or close friend?
   __ To purposely talk and share things on your heart
   __ To just listen and support the other person
   __ To rekindle rapport and discuss future goals or dreams.

4. Are you making family time a priority?
   __ Schedule family time on a weekly or regular basis
   __ Plan outings, events, or vacations together
   __ Have fun making memories together with simple things and special retreats

5. Can you remind yourself daily of ways to do unto others as you want them to do unto you?
   __ Be respectful to the other person even if it's challenging
   __ Encourage and compliment people when you get the opportunity
   __ Make special efforts to be generous to others

CHAPTER SEVEN

It's All in Your Head—MINDSET

Mindset is the set of beliefs a person has, and these beliefs determine how they view life and the world. Some believe that mindset involves all of one's five senses: taste, touch, sight, smell, and hearing. Our mindset is created over the course of experiences and surroundings and dictates our trajectory in life. In this chapter, we will discover how developing and maintaining a *growth* mindset is vital to recovering from burnout.

The word *growth* was added to mindset some thirty-plus years ago by psychologist Carol Dweck of Stanford University. The term was birthed as a standard after she created the phrase in her book, *Mindset, The New Psychology of Success*. She traveled to schools and playgrounds and studied children, noting that individuals who have a growth mindset are the ones who believe in themselves and strive to become better through learning, helping others, and working hard themselves.[26]

A person with a growth mindset does not settle for the status quo. They want to achieve and be all they can be in life. This

---

26 "What Is a Growth Mindset? 8 Steps to Develop One." 2019. WGU North Carolina; part of Western Governors University.

man or woman reaches for the stars. They may or may not have a personal mission statement or a vision plan, but they are achievers wanting to constantly learn and improve themselves. The person with a growth mindset is always learning, growing, achieving, and excelling in the gifts and talents already in place.

No one is perfect, but each of us is unique in our abilities and talents. Comparing ourselves with someone else does not work, and we should be careful of the comparison game. It's an unwinnable game. The winning result from having a growth mindset is for each person to become the best *they* can become, not in comparison to anyone else.

We must look at our mindset because it contains the key to our growth and future accomplishments. It is easy to get caught up in the vacuum of everything becoming stale and lifeless. We get tired, push to excel, and sometimes feel like we have failed. A good ole reality check is essential to not getting stuck in mediocrity.

A *fixed* mindset is when a person convinces themselves that they must remain satisfied with where they are in personal growth. Thoughts come such as, *I will never get any better at this than I am now.* Or, *I have reached the pinnacle of my talents and abilities.* Come on, now, you just got stuck and doomed yourself to doing the same ole, same ole. I get stuck sometimes and lose my joy and focus. When a lack of growth in my life is apparent, I immediately acknowledge that I have fallen into a fixed mindset.

Living with a fixed mindset is like accepting a bad bed partner. You and I must be convinced that we can always grow. Learn to give yourself some space to moan and groan, but do not stay in the fixed thinking position. Look outside the box and see great things you want to experience and/or accomplish, and motivation can begin to lead you toward renewed growth.

Be honest with yourself. If you are in a stalemate, do something positive about it. The next section should help get the ball rolling.

How Do I Develop a Growth Mindset?

There are many ways to foster and improve our growth mindset. Next I'll share a few ways you can begin improving yourself.

1. *Make a conscious effort.*

   Look for ways to grow and be positive about a fresh way to think and achieve. You are not in a race with anyone. Take gradual steps to think about growth, maturity, and development.

2. *Speak to yourself with positive words.*

   Positivity fuels growth in our minds, which equates to our mindset and resulting actions. This may be a new voice to you, but it encourages your purpose. Think *I can*, instead of *I can't*. Your positive words will stand up strong against negative feelings. Inner motivation is imperative to achieve and succeed.

3. *Know that you always have a choice.*

   We need to keep a careful ear to ourselves. Ask yourself, "Which voice am I listening to?" Slow down and be keenly aware of your choice to grow or be lazy. Choose well!

4. *Learn from others, but be who you are.*

   It is extremely easy and natural to seek the approval of others. All of us need some outside help in many areas of life. Others can push us forward by mentoring and advising. Remember that you must give an account to yourself, so make your focus on your growth, desires, and dreams.

You are aware of the challenges of having a growth mindset, so get started, perhaps in baby steps. Focus on your objectives. Be prepared to stop and reset. It is always good to check up on our goals and progress. Sometimes it will be important to reestablish our direction and focus. Stay fresh in your approach. Keep the positive talk going and cultivate your mindset.

Working on Your Growth

A growth mindset develops when you understand that you can develop skills in areas above your gifts or talents. That is what a growth mindset can bring. It is not about being talented in a certain area of life, but rather believing that you can become talented in a new capacity any time you choose. You can learn to paint portraits, fish, be creative, and play a musical instrument.

Carol Dweck's journeys in schools landed her in a conversation with a seven-year-old girl who gave her this impressive quote. The girl said, "I think intelligence is something you have to work for. It isn't just given to you... If they're not sure of an answer, most kids will not raise their hand to answer the question. But what I usually do is raise my hand because if I'm wrong, my mistake will be corrected. Or I will raise my hand and say, 'How would this be solved?' or 'I don't get this. Can you help me?' Just by doing that, I'm increasing my intelligence."[27]

As leaders, we tend to think of the best for others, and we should. But if we are not careful, we will place ourselves on the back burner to our detriment. To think of others first, you must have a true alignment of number one, you. If you are not growing your leadership or skills, you will be unable to lead your team through the growth of inevitable change in any environment.

We have all heard it said, "Leaders are readers." I believe that is a true statement. If you and I do not read, we stop growing. We

---

27 Tuck, Anthony. 2021. "Mindset and Identity." RedPropeller Speakers Bureau.

get stuck in the mud and left behind. I have multiple college degrees. I have read myself crazy, and upon studying each class and the endeavor of reading each book, I am always enlightened. The more I learn, the more I recognize how much I do not know. Find the greatest books or authors in the arena of your profession and read their books. Read good articles, research the internet to your heart's desire, and read good books.

Replace Negative with Positive

Have you ever noticed that bad news about someone travels rapidly? And good news will travel at a slower pace and usually fizzles out quickly? Negativity is powerfully damaging to our growth mindset. Replacing the negative with positive elements is imperative. We should strive to grow, and being motivated for positive growth will excite us about who we are and what we do.

There are many ways to approach our subject, but I want to give you some things that you can easily embrace. The bottom line is this. *Your attitude determines your altitude.* Being negative will make you fail. You can't deliver positive results with a negative attitude.

Let us use simple tools to accomplish replacing negative things with positive actions:

- Change a habit—get out of your rut.
- Find a trusted friend and bring them on the journey with you.
- Stop that thought—prevent a negative thought from grabbing you and pulling you down.
- Slow down, think about it again, breathe, respond. Act purposefully and do not react.
- Talk to yourself with positive words of encouragement.

- Find some good uplifting music and start all over.
- Accept yourself and give yourself some margin for error (and correcting your errors). Rehearse this often.
- You are the one who must take control of your thoughts.
- Remember that you are a winner, you are a leader, you are the only you.
- Remind yourself that your thoughts are only thoughts and they are not you.

Practice Makes Perfect, or Almost Perfect

We all know by personal experience that it takes work to stay positive. We all fail at being Patricia or Paul the Positive because none of us is perfect. Practice will make us better. We will succeed more often when we try more often. Don't just try, try hard.

I want to note that we should not make it too hard on ourselves but should be accountable to ourselves and someone else. You know as well as I do that people who succeed in life are the ones who practice personal discipline. It is difficult to be disciplined, but winners make the sacrifice to say yes or no to certain things so they can maintain good habits and be effective in achieving their goals. Sometimes, it's saying no to certain foods, drinks, bad habits, wrong company, lack of exercise, staying up late, getting up too early, or damaging addictions that helps us replace negatives with positives. Here are some points to practice while developing your growth mindset:

- Practice saying no to yourself and others.
- Have fun making a difference with a new challenge.
- Set time limits for things that you know can get out of hand.

- Have goals and deadline dates.
- Only begin a new project when you have completed the last one.
- Reward yourself when you have finished a job, task, or a special deadline.

Self-awareness is a key element for working on our mindset and personal growth. Put it all together: Invest in you, replace negative with positive, and practice makes perfect. These exercises can move us to the best version of ourselves.

Learn to Love People Again

Getting burned from a hot burner on the stove is usually a painful warning to not let that happen again. We become conscious of the aching and ouch of a burn. Because we pull back and become cautious of things that hurt us, we use the same type of painful warning signs in other areas of life. Being emotionally burned as a reward for loving and caring for people can also prevent us from loving other people, and harboring these feelings can be detrimental to a positive growth mindset.

Love can be like a limb on a tree. If we climb onto a limb and the limb breaks with us, we will tumble to the ground. We experience pain or brokenness and don't want to get out on a limb again. We tend to carry this type of mental pain into broken relationships with people we have cared for, helped, and loved. Practice what you learned about forgiveness and then learn to love people again.

Trust people with the concept of *handling relationships loosely*. In other words, accept that each person will probably not always be in your life. This also goes for family members. We are not guaranteed how many years we will be alive, so remember that loved ones and friendships are temporary. Holding things loosely is not the mindset that you are waiting for someone to lie to you or let you down. Holding people and relationships loosely allows you to trust who you are as a person no matter what you lose. Remember what we learned about resentment, guilt, and bitterness or blame. Having a growth mindset must include this aspect as well because any negativity in our minds will work against the positive results we're aiming for.

Learning to love and trust others begins with *baby steps:*

- Give the person a chance; allow them the benefit of the doubt.
- Spend time together and share thoughts and beliefs to get to know them all over again.
- Begin to believe in the person.
- Start trusting but hold things loosely.
- Discuss with the other person about working on this concept with you.

We live a healthy psychological life when we employ the view that people, in general, are not our enemies. We are all flawed, messed up, and need love and guidance. Yes, as I have previously noted, we all need counseling at various times.

Marcie Arie, a marketing director, suffered burnout midway through her career. She tells the story of her own difficulty to love people again. She stated, "I poured my entire life into people and a company that ended with me being treated like a replaceable number." Marcie had been lied about and sabotaged by others who wanted her position and prestige. These things on top of the mental stress and fatigue of her role catapulted her into burnout. She was discarded by her supervisors in the process. After a battle of mental brokenness and burnout that lasted five years, she agonized over the wounds of having to retire early from a career she once loved. Marcie received counseling and developed a growth plan, on which she has now been working for several years. She is growing in her ability to trust people and love people again. Marcie said, "I realize that love is a choice, and I am choosing to love people again one at a time."

Loving people is more than a feeling, it is a positive choice. We can all acknowledge that some people are downright difficult to love. Wouldn't it be awesome if people were not so stupid? Oh, wait, you and I are *people*. I admit that I have done some stupid, not so wise things. All of us do things that do not sit well with others. We have all hurt people either unintentionally or intentionally. Thus, just as we would want someone to give us a second chance, and maybe a third or fourth, we should be willing to do the same for others. Do unto others, remember?

When you think about it, love is a choice we make each day of our lives. Love is a commitment, especially in a marriage. Since love is more than a feeling and more of a choice, it is important to remember that you are vulnerable with your feelings when choosing to love. Choosing to love someone has nothing to do with agreeing with their addictions or wrongs they commit. Love does mean that I will help you the best that I can and I am here for you when you fall.

When you and I choose to love, we need to remember that sometimes loving people gets messy. Love will ask us to do the hard things. This type of love is extremely challenging to any individual who has gone through burnout.

One of the most blessed ways to make a positive choice and love people is to get out of your comfort zone. Getting out of your comfort zone positions you to *pay it forward*, through which your positive growth mindset can flourish. Here's how:

Volunteer in your community.
- Choose a cause you can be passionate about. Look around in your community for needs to be met, like working with

victims of unfortunate circumstances, underprivileged children, or the local community center. Find your passion and pursue it.

- Spend some time at a local animal shelter. Many animal shelters welcome residents to help in various ways. If you love animals, volunteering at a facility can be rewarding.

- Donate blood. You can make it an event either by yourself or with your family, or with a group of friends. Donating blood is a sacrificial event that can save lives.

- Serve at a food pantry or a food kitchen. It is fulfilling to connect with people from other walks of life and bad circumstances that vary from your own. You can inspire some smiles on those who have gone through much pain while gaining perspective on your own struggles.

- Provide help at your church or a community charitable organization. There are always fun prospects of serving people in many ways at church services or community events.

- Give your assistance in tutoring or mentoring students. You can volunteer at a private or public school. After a background check, you can be on your way to bringing support to students who need the extra care and using your creativity to make a difference in some young lives.

- Encourage the elderly. You will find volunteering at an assisted living community or a senior nursing facility a blessing and an encouragement to yourself as you give a smile and sense of renewed life to confined residents.

- Donate your books or used clothing and merchandise. Do not store everything away for the varmints to chew on. Give it to an organization that will ensure the items are used by some who will appreciate them.

- Use your coaching skills. You may have sports coaching skills or nurturing skills that can provide needed assistance to many people. Once again, follow your passion and locate the right place for you to serve and train others.

If you are looking for a way to get out of that comfort zone and use your life to give life and happiness to other people, there are many more ways than what has been listed. Be creative and look for ways to bless, love, and encourage people who need what you have to offer.

Byron S. was tired of trying to care about people. Over a period of twenty-plus years, he was the senior project manager in several organizations. He led companies to growth and prosperity in a short time frame in all of his positions. But with each organization he worked with, some of those who had been there before him felt threatened by the changes he brought. The threat was compounded by the organization's growth and success. They could not rejoice in the company prospering, so rumors, lies, and divisions were birthed. Byron, being the agent for change, became the scapegoat. Finally, the constant battling with the old guard and self-doubt led Byron to a complete mental breakdown. This breakdown was so severe that it led to a month under psychiatric care.

Several years after he got his life and family back to some normalcy, he knew that he had talents to be used in caring for and blessing people. As anyone could understand, Byron did not want to step out on that limb again and have the limb break with him on it. Over several years, he and his family moved a couple of different times. A friend hired him and his wife to operate his insurance company. A lady who was a fellow employee invited them to visit her church. The church was new, and they met in a school. Byron and his family had visited many churches in the area. However, his fear and still tender scars led him to find fault and excuses not to return in every church. His wife encouraged him to try one more time and attend church with the lady from work. After visiting the church, to his surprise, he liked the authenticity of the church and became a regular attender. After a few months of attending, becoming a member, and serving in that church, he became one of its pastors. At the time of writing his story, he is still employed on the church staff. A person can love and care again, but it has to be their choice.

Eight Tips to Feel Like Caring Again

To keep on loving, a person must look beyond themselves. Look beyond your insecurities and your hurts to provide smiles and gratitude in the lives of those less fortunate than yourself. If you have lost your desire to care for others, there is no judgment coming from me. However, there is a time to get back out. There is a time to stop playing a victim and use your God-given talents, abilities, and unique skill sets to help someone else find their dream. You're missing out on experiences that will further your own growth mindset and help you fulfill your purpose in life.

Allow me to provide you with some thought-provoking ways to *feel like caring again.*

- Start the day off positively. Decide that no matter what, the day will be a good day. Read what encourages you or listen to uplifting music. Get yourself in a good frame of mind to be on purpose.
- Count your blessings. It is always beneficial to stop and be grateful for what you have. Many people have it worse in their life than you do today. When you feel like everything around you is negative, stop and write a column of blessings and good things: people, health, family, and friends.

- Be aware of all the people who have helped you. None of us is an island. We all have reached pinnacles in life because someone gave us a chance and believed in us. Someone needs you to believe in them—find them and bless them today.

- Purposely speak positive self-talk. Speak self-talk in positive ways. If you embrace the positive, you can spill positive words, smiles, and actions over into others. The opposite of that will only pull you and others down.

- Learn from your mess-ups. You and I can be so down on people that we forget we have had some royal mess-ups in our own lives. Learn from the mess-ups and give others margin and grace being just as human as you are.

- Speak kindly and watch the different responses. Just try it. Find ways to speak words of inspiration to people and watch their reactions. Who knows, perhaps you are some person's divine appointment for that day. Someone's life may have fallen apart before you saw them at the grocery store, restaurant, or job.

- Hang out with positive people. You know it's true that you become like the people you run with. Find ways to be around positive people instead of those who drag everyone with them into the pit of despair. Find positive people and allow their lives to rub good, healthy, and positive values off on you.

- Pay for someone's coffee, a meal at the restaurant, or groceries of the person in line behind you. If you have ever had anyone pay for your lunch, groceries, or coffee, you know the feeling of gratitude this inspires. We could all share stories of being blessed or having blessed someone completely unaware of the generosity of a kind person.

These action tips can generate feelings of caring for people and lead us to a happy heart. Please tell me, who does not like that? I want that, and if you dig deep inside, you will also admit that you want to be the kind of person who cares for others again. Be brave and take these steps one at a time and one day at a time.

Exercise:
Foster Your Growth Mindset

To foster our mindset, it is important to turn negative thoughts into positive thinking. Below you will find examples of how to turn a negative mindset into a positive action. Make these exercises your own by replacing these examples with your own thoughts and situations.

Negative Mindset: I can never lead my staff to reach our monthly project deadlines.

Growth Mindset: I am going to explore ways to use the strengths of my staff to reach our monthly project deadlines.

Negative Mindset: My personal financial situation is impossible to overcome.

Growth Mindset: I am beginning to improve my financial situation by seriously noting my spending habits and applying any extra money to paying off one thing at a time.

Negative Mindset: Burnout took me into a dark place, and I'm afraid that I will never recover.

Growth Mindset: Burnout set me back, but I am applying myself to heal and become mentally whole.

Negative Mindset: My relationships always turn into a disaster.

Growth Mindset: I am working on relationship skills to improve my connections with others.

Negative Mindset: Since I am getting older, my company may suspect that I am less valuable to the team.

Growth Mindset: Age can become a factor on the job, but I work hard to stay current in working with technology and job skills.

Negative Mindset: I fear burning out again.

Growth Mindset: I never want to experience burning out a second time, so I have put into place techniques to keep me accountable, growing, and aware so I will never burn out again.

Chapter Eight
A Personal Growth 90-Day Plan

I want to take a moment to tell you how proud I am of you for taking this voyage with me to move from brokenness and burnout to a life of health and wholeness again. Now we are on the home stretch. We're going to walk through a few simple exercises to help you stretch and learn more about yourself than maybe you have ever known. To challenge you to keep growing in your personal life, we will look at a simple 90-day commitment divided into three 30-day segments. As you work your way through the burnout healing process, I invite you to enjoy life again and keep on growing!

What I will share with you contains some dynamics to drive you. Each 30-day segment will grow you and stretch you to be the best you possible. These suggestions are not what you might think of as important for men. Yes, I said men. You might think this is women's stuff, not to segregate anyone. This book is non-gender-specific, is for everyone who has been a leader or desires to lead. So, gentlemen, please allow your invisible wall of manhood or stereotype-thinking to be open so you too can renew and grow. You are at a different place in life today than you were before burnout.

Your first thirty days will be to journal. If you have never journaled, you are in for a treat. If you have followed a journal plan, this one will be different. As previously stated, you are in a different place in your life now. You are healing mentally, and you want to move into life with more joy and freedom than you have ever considered possible. Enjoy!

We will first look at *what, why, and how* to journal.

Your Journal—The First Thirty Days

The What

To my recollection, I first began to journal seventeen years ago. Today, I journal occasionally and more often when I need clarity and stress relief. It doesn't need to be an organized process—just write. Organize your thoughts and get them out of your head. Try various ways of getting your thoughts out. There is no right or wrong way. Just be you and do something that will be enjoyable and emotionally healthy. Remember, your words are for your eyes only, so you have nothing to lose.

The Why

The process of writing or typing about feelings, anxieties, or life considerations is a healthy mental exercise that helps us process better, faster, more effectively than just letting our thoughts run wild. Journaling helps you get thoughts from the mind onto paper so you can see them. It can be amazing and revealing to see your thoughts from this different viewpoint. I prefer to hand write when I journal, but it can be done so many ways. The things you write can be questions, heart yearnings, or even prayers you place for your benefit. When a person writes, types, or records the things in their mind, it allows them to pour out spontaneous thoughts purposely. I and many others have found the exercise therapeutic.

Once you have begun the journaling process, you will later have the privilege of going back at any time and reading the thoughts of your heart. It can be rewarding to go back for days, weeks, months, or years to read what was going on in your life and see how things worked out and what you learned from it.

The How

Set a time to journal and stick to your schedule. Many people find morning to be the best time to think, when first starting the day. Do not be too rigid with yourself but determine to set aside a time and stick to it for thirty days. By journaling for thirty days, you will find out more about yourself and what is going on inside your mind beyond your imagination. Journaling can be mental cleansing, which is something we all need from time to time. So much is going on in our lives, and each of us requires mental recharging.

Journaling does not have to be on paper. The key is to be self-aware. Some people like to write out their feelings or desires while others enjoy typing because they can type faster than handwriting. Some find a mental release by drawing or sketching stick figures. Perhaps you want to talk it out and voice record your thoughts. From time to time, change your process up.

Start easy. Take small steps. The first day or two, you might sit there thinking you have nothing to say, write, or record. There is no wrong way to do this. Try journaling in whatever form you desire and only do it in ten-minute segments. Give yourself achievable goals so you can assure your success.

Try thinking of gratitude when you journal. A journal should *not* be just a daily personal gripe session. There will be days that the journal's focus will be on pain and hurt, but no one wants to live there. By thinking of gratitude, you will pull out the positives of your life that will in turn help your mental state become more positive. Perhaps divide your paper into two columns with headings: Pain and Pleasure. Then you can see the good things in your life. Recognizing good can help move gloom out of the way.

The healthy part of journaling is in the vulnerability and honesty that you give yourself in the act. Be transparent with yourself. Being open and real is the true solution to gaining peace and tranquility.

It is important to find the way or ways that motivate you best, that are conducive to doing the work, and referring to it in useful growth mindset ways. It may be wise to try a few different methods until you find the right fit for yourself. Be creative.

Be mindful of how you are doing with your journal. Things to continue or things to avoid. Ask yourself, "How is journaling helping me?" Be aware of your emotions. Consciously do what is necessary to make your 30-day journaling work for you. When you complete the thirty days, you may have discovered your way of recording fresh insights into your life or that this one-time thirty-day event is okay but not for you.

Let me suggest getting someone to keep you accountable with the 30-day plan. We are looking for some healing and personal growth. Do not get lazy on yourself; you are worth more than the mediocrity that can easily set in if you allow yourself to be lazy about it.

At the end of your 30-day journal, sit down and process and evaluate how you feel and how this has helped you. Most people who give it an honest try find a release and blessing. Some people attempt to journal and never try it again. I have found that those who make the thirty-day attempt receive more out of the process than they ever thought possible. Go for it and find someone to help you stay accountable to complete this goal once more. You've got this thing! Enjoy your first piece of the pie.

Your Vision Board—The Second Thirty Days

Congratulations, you are now ready to move onto your second thirty-day segment. It sounds corny to some, but it can be a lot of fun and quite fulfilling. Once again, men, please do not cheat yourself of growth and a vision blessing. A vision board sounds foreign to us guys. I proclaim that you are in for a treat, though. Just follow through with me and see for yourself.

Archie Wayne, a business owner and contractor, said after doing this exercise, "I was so hesitant to attempt anything like a vision board. It just was not me. Only when I was placed in a have-to situation did I compile my first vision board. I was in a leadership training seminar, and each participant had to create a vision board. I felt almost sick to my stomach and wanted to hide in the restroom, but I knew I could not do that. I followed the trainer's instructions and began the process, laying out pieces of what seemed like a puzzle. Shortly, all of it began to make sense, and I started having fun. I was finding names, words, pictures, and quotes of things that related to the five things that I needed to glue on a poster board. As soon as I completed the project, I felt so much accomplishment because my vision board allows me to see it daily and encourages me to stay on track."

My first opportunity to make a vision board was in a certification class, and we had only one hour to create our boards. Man, I felt pressured, but I had so much fun and the process brought great happiness. I could visualize my goals, dreams, and life pursuit on one white poster board for the first time. Since then, I have reviewed, worked, and updated my vision board many times.

I promise you that working on a vision board is one of the most simple and gratifying projects you will have ever done.

The What and the How of a Vision Board

The "what" of the vision board is a simple concept. A vision board contains a collection of words, sentences, phrases, and pictures that a person puts together on a poster board to describe their dreams, goals, or life vision. The backing holding the items is unimportant; it can be almost anything. Poster board, a door, a wall, or a refrigerator can be used. Some people make digital vision boards.

The board containing your vision should clearly represent what you are trying to accomplish and is supposed to connect and help individuals keep their goals focused. The whole idea is not to add stress or give you something else to add to your to-do list. The goal is to map out and visualize your dreams so you can follow through with them. The board should add to your excitement for living and give you more reason to pursue good things. Remember that your vision for your board can be flexible and you can always change or modify things to better suit you personally.

Here's how to get started:

1. Make a list of personal goals or personal dreams on a notepad or a piece of paper. You can have one month, six months, one year, three years, and so on for the vision board. Relax and just structure it the best way that feels right for you.

2. Decide which goal is first and write that down. Then list the next and the next goal, dream, or achievement. You might jot down up to your top four to five goals, etc. These will eventually be placed on your board, but only after you finish mapping your thoughts out in a logical order. You may want to include goals you did not accomplish in the past year, but it is not necessary.

3. Now divide your items into categories, such as:
    - Work achievements

- Business ventures
- Entrepreneur goals
- Family and time with the family
- Vacation dreams, planning, and saving
- Hobbies
- Health or wellness, mental and physical
- Opportunities for growth

Once you have the basic structure that makes the most sense for you mapped out, you are ready to begin the process of creating your board. Make it fun! You will need a supply list with items such as:

- Board material: poster, wall, door, or digital board
- Magazines, newspapers, pamphlets, etc.
- Scissors
- Glue sticks
- Newspapers
- Tape
- Markers—all the colors that you want in life

Now, let's put it all together:

1. Begin cutting out words, pictures, phrases, and statements that tell the story of your vision or dream. Take your time on this step and be thorough to capture all the imagery you can for illustrating your visions. You can have your spouse, partner, child, or a friend assist you with this life-giving project. Make an evening or afternoon event out of it.

2. Lay out and organize your board with the cuttings and pictures. Refer to your notes and place your items in the arrange-

ment on your board that makes the most sense of your dreams or vision. You can tape or paste them once you have them in place.

Some people separate their board by categories, but if you have one big goal, perhaps placing the items for that goal in the center and all the other goals around it would work best for you. Do it *your* way, and that will be the *best* way. Whatever flips your switch, do it. Make the board speak to you to enable you to visualize all the areas of your life that you want on your vision board. Be creative and have fun! You've got this!

What Now?

You have your board complete, so *where* do you place it and *what* do you do now? If you have created a portable vision board, place your board where you will see it daily. You need the reminder, and the more you take notice of your board, the more your subconscious mind will develop a truer mental picture of the imagery. If you created your vision board on your computer, print a copy, perhaps enlarge it, and then post it up where you will almost stumble over it regularly.

Next, use your board to:

- Reflect on your goals and dreams daily
- Repeat your goals aloud
- Imagine yourself taking steps toward each goal
- Choose the first goal or dream and begin working on it
- Set a time and date for completing the goal
- Set an accountability plan for each effort toward achieving a goal

This step of creating your vision board is a thirty-day project, though you can complete it as quickly as you wish. It will take time to gather all the items to illustrate your board, and you will want to plan a day or an hour here and there to work on it.

I hope that you will not only attempt to create your vision board but complete the task. The thought process and work will move you forward toward making a positive difference in your life.

Sharing Your Journey—The Third Thirty Days

Sharing can be reviving and redeeming. As you sailed through the first thirty days of journaling, something special was happening within you. The second thirty days of creating your vision board opened things up again, allowing you to see life as full of grand opportunities. The third stretch of your voyage will allow you to dig a little deeper into sharing your journey. We often forget that when we share, we grow and receive fulfillment.

The seventeenth-century English poet and dean of St. Paul's Cathedral in London England, John Donne, made a statement in his Seventeenth Meditation (from his *Devotions Upon Emergent Occasions*). Most of us have read or heard someone quote the statement made by the master scholar, poet, and soldier that goes like this: "No man is an island."[28]

I am sure there may be many ways to think about this statement. The context of his statement was human connection. Donne expressed the need that humanity has for relationships with other people, as such relationships are necessary for our survival and well-being.

When we share stories and knowledge of our lives with another person, we don't intend to receive the blessing. We are trying to help and bless that person. The crazy thing is, when we bless someone, we get a blessing too.

---

28 Tearle, Dr. Oliver. 2022. "A Short Analysis of John Donne's 'No Man Is an Island' Meditation." Interesting Literature.

- *When we share our lives, we rediscover how blessed we are.* Sometimes we forget to count our blessings when we are caught up by life situations.
- *When we share our lives, we are reminded of our passion.* Passion is often pushed to the back shelf in our minds when there are events that crowd the closet of our minds. Sharing can revive our calling or our passion.
- *When we share our lives, we feel the spark inside that our story is powerful.* Don't we forget the power of purpose and the powerful effect our lives have on people?
- *When we share our lives, vulnerabilities, and imperfections, we make it easier for others to make a connection with us.* People do not connect with perfection but rather the opposite. People are drawn to someone who acknowledges their feet of clay. Most of us relate to a person who reveals their flaws more than a person who hides behind a wall of success. Success is great, yet we realize the blunders and setbacks were the building blocks to the wins in life and prefer to connect with people who know this too.

Sharing can be reviving and redeeming each time you and I become transparent and pour our lives into a person who is open and responsive. We step out, instruct, and encourage someone, and when they grasp what we have shared, we grow to another level in our maturity. Keep sharing with others. Sometimes we must almost fight or battle against ourselves to reach out to love and bless others. As we have discussed, we tend to withdraw when we get burned or hurt by relationships. Let's face it, who wants to get burned or wounded again? No one. As we heal, there is a time to step out and love, mentor others, to share our journey with someone.

Someone once told me never to *waste a hurt*. Think about those words: never—waste – hurt. I think you understand what I am saying. Someone has hurt you. I have been hurt by someone, and all human creation has been hurt by someone. Imagine if all of humanity withdrew and said, "I will never give anyone a chance to hurt me again, never again!" Life as we know it would cease to exist.

You have gone through tough, painful, and traumatizing situations. Many people are going through similar things. Many will travel common paths. You have a great deal to share.

Think of the person or persons who you will be able to put your hand on their shoulder and then say, "I know exactly how you feel." When you share your emotions and wisdom, people who are hurting will find comfort and assurance. Sharing can be healing and liberating to both the giver and the recipient. Sharing is caring.

Your story is amazing, personal, and unique. This is why you can make a huge difference in the life of someone else. Many people can benefit from you and your story. There are many lonely people within a stone's throw from you and me. I like to think of it as when I reach out to be generous to someone who needs someone to care, my life is helping them to feel less lonely.

I have had many mentors, some of them direct but most indirect. I believe that we only live this life one time, so we have only one chance to make a difference in the lives of the living. I believe that you, like me, want your life to count big. Each day of living is a blessing, even when we have days we may consider a disaster or a curse. I want us to rethink and perhaps repurpose the concept of making a difference in the life or lives of others.

- *Make a difference in the life of some who has been crying their guts out.* There is much pain in the lives of many hurting people. Pain that was inflicted upon them and pain they imposed upon themselves.

- *Make a difference in the life of someone just starting.* I don't want to look at someone newly struggling and think, *Well, I had to learn on my own the hard way, so let them struggle through it.* While there are many things we must learn ourselves, some people are open to ideas and suggestions to help them navigate things. If your life experience can give a person a three- or six-month head start, you have given them something money cannot buy.

- *Making a difference in the life of someone can inspire them to do great things.* There are many someones who are just about to quit. They are ready to give up and throw in the towel. You can make a difference in that person's life, and your words and the life you have lived can inspire them to try another day or another week or month. They will be given the right time to move beyond their current obstacle.

Hip-hip and hoorah, you are on the edge of completing your journey to life after leadership burnout. Thank you for voyaging with me! There have been many hurdles in the process, and maybe some of my suggestions felt impossible to accomplish. Well, I know that you can do it. And you can always revisit any area you struggled with, read through it all again, discard what doesn't resonate with you, and so on. Use what works for you so you are doing something to make positive moves forward in your journey to heal and recover from burnout.

I am still with you, and many people believe in you and will continue to support you. You are a winner. You are greatly important and triumphant. Mark this page and come back and read it often.

Exercise:
30-, 60-, & 90-Day Growth Plan

The First Thirty Days—Your Journal
- Just write whatever is on your mind, spontaneous thoughts.
- Write heartfelt words you would like to say to someone.
- Draw, if you can express yourself that way.
- Write about your day yesterday.
- Write your prayers to God.
- Jot down goals and things that motivate you.
- Note all the ways you want to bless or help others.
- Make your journal messy and personal, capturing a true version of what's going on inside of you.

The Second Thirty Days—Your Vision Board
- Make a list of your goals and dreams on paper.
- Create your vision board using cutouts from magazines, newspapers, pamphlets, etc.
- Glue or tape these items to map out your goals and dreams.
- Place your board in a highly visible location and refer to it regularly.
- Use your board daily, repeat goals, imagine each step, and be accountable to your vision.

The Third Thirty Days—Sharing Your Journey
- Bless and encourage others by sharing your dreams.
- Be accountable with someone to help you stay on track with working toward your vision.
- Make a difference in someone else's life by the example of your life changes.

CHAPTER NINE

Your Amazing Story

We have voyaged together through *Leadership Burnout and Recovery (From One Who Was Burned Out and Broken)* on our journey from brokenness to wholeness. I have been able to write this book because I, just like you, have personally lived it. As captain of our ship, I made you a promise at the very beginning of this book.

> *While principles provided in this writing are primarily for the burned-out to regain mental wholeness, you and I can practice the same teachings to prevent burnout and stop it in its early stages.*

Please incorporate these principles that we walked through together and spread the love to any friend, relative, or work associate you know who needs to hear it.

You have a story to live and tell, and it's your blessing. I want to encourage you from the depths of my heart to put your boots back on and get back up on the horse. You may or may not continue in your profession, but remember that you are not your job. Your job is something that you do. Again, please do not consider yourself a victim, because you are a victor!

As you continue your amazing journey through life, I want to inspire you to place the past brokenness and burnout into history. Do not miss this—your painful experience of burnout should not occupy the forefront of your mind. File it away as history you can learn from and help others learn from, as I have done for you. Nobody deserves to stay in the past, and neither should anyone remain a victim. Yes, I said that again.

The wise leader takes burnout of the past and places reminders in their memory bank to never allow stress or anxiety to take them down that path again. We learn burnout triggers and practice restorative measures to learn coping skills.

I want you to pay close attention to the burnout story of Levi, who is dear to me. As a young man making his way in the corporate world as a senior manager in a nationwide commercial construction company, burnout led him into a living hell. It devastated his life and nearly plunged him to utter destruction.

Levi tells his story:

> When I used to think of someone experiencing burnout, I would associate that with being weak. I felt that if someone had a breakdown or became burned out, they were somehow reduced and didn't have what it took until it happened to me. My burnout experience and how I handled it sent my life into a tailspin until it inevitably took a nosedive to rock bottom.
>
> In my midtwenties, I was doing well financially. I worked hard, made good financial decisions, and had substantial money in the bank. I had a career, two houses, a sports car, a truck, and

a motorcycle. I realize that it's not extravagant compared to some, but I am painting a picture that possessions and money had become important to me and my relationship. Work had become so demanding that I never truly had a consistent day off. I became overly stressed and started to experience anxiety at work and home. Taking time off for vacations caused more issues than it was worth, and the thought of dealing with it created more stress. My direct management at work was demanding, and customers were challenging. I would have a migraine by midmorning every day at work, and I became mentally exhausted. Eventually, I started experiencing severe anxiety and was put on medication to treat it. I also began having other health issues for which I saw specialists, and I was put on multiple other medications. It felt like I couldn't find an escape and was burned out in most areas of my life. Burning at both ends, I knew it would take drastic changes to relieve stress, and I felt stuck. I could not keep up at work, I no longer found joy in my hobbies, and I didn't want to be involved with social activities like I once did.

Sometime before all of this, I learned that I received mental relief while taking prescription pain medication during a physical injury. I didn't realize it at the time, but I was looking for something to help me cope with the stresses of life. It was a monumental mistake to begin to self-medicate and think I had it all under control. I started taking substances during the weekend to relax and unwind. After all, I deserved to take a break, right? Not only did I like the way it made me feel, but I found out it helped me work with more concentration. I could work longer, faster, and accomplish more.

My relationship at home seemed more fulfilling, and I became more social. It felt like a no-brainer. Quickly it became a situation in which I wasn't only doing it during the weekend, but I had certain days I would use during the week. Maybe I needed an extra boost for a project on Wednesday, and then I might talk myself into having a feel-good Friday. I could accomplish all my tasks on Friday and even start the weekend early. "Besides, it's not like I do this every week," I would tell myself. The better I felt, the more I took. The more I took, the more I had to take. It wasn't long before my drug use went from recreational to a daily addiction. From the time I woke up to when I went to bed, I had to use it so that I could sleep.

Secretly my addiction spun out of control, and I had a habit that was costing me thousands of dollars a week and six figures a year. I was rapidly depleting my savings and any income coming in; I knew it could not continue financially, and something had to change. I attempted to get clean and be done with it, but that didn't last long. In fact, I picked up another addiction in the process. Now I was no longer working consistently, and I had to rent out my house. My world was crashing down around me, and I had done it to myself. I found myself selling personal possessions and not paying bills so that

I could afford to feed my addiction. I wanted to give up, no longer wanting to live, being disgusted with myself, and needing money.

Embarrassed and ashamed, there were times that I contemplated ending it all. I thought I would never find joy in life again, and I thought I was worthless. I was miserable, and I expected to die.

I started to hang out with some rough people that did violent things to provide for themselves. Grasping at straws, I even did certain acts that could have landed me in prison for a long time. God especially protected me during these times. Unrelated, I encountered some legal issues after being arrested and accumulating a few charges. While out of jail on bail and awaiting my court date, which was six months away, I still could not manage to stay clean. So much so that I took substances with me to my final court date and somehow managed not to get caught with it. I was a mess. The plea bargain agreement I took to keep from going to jail required a couple of years of probation, and a result of that was close to a year of required intensive outpatient treatment. At the time, I thought this was awful, but little did I know this was a blessing in disguise. I had lost almost everything, and somehow, that wasn't enough for me to turn things around. Now I faced prison time if I did not make a change. Thankfully, this accountability, combined with my family never giving up on me, led me to finally get clean and stay clean. I learned some healthy coping skills and how to watch my stress and anxiety levels. It still is and will always be a process.

I hurt a lot of people during those years. My close friends and family took the brunt of the hurt. The sleepless nights of not knowing where I was or what I was doing. As I stood in front of the mirror and looked into my eyes, I knew I wasn't myself. Words will never explain what I put my loved ones through, the damage I caused, and how sorry I am for it. All I can do is be the best version of myself now and make them proud. Thanks to everyone who stood by my side through the ups and downs, and I love you. Today I am over six years clean and happily married, and at times I get to help people and allow God to use my experience to relate to what they or their family members might be going through. I once again have things I enjoy doing, and I look forward to living, which I thought was never possible again.

My burnout experience started small, but I allowed it to escalate into a destructive path that destroyed me. I became someone completely different, someone I did not recognize. After all, I thought it could never happen to me because I was better than that.

If you feel that you are approaching burnout, be aware of that and watch it closely. Make a change before it changes you. Burnout doesn't care who you are or what your status is. It can sneak up on you and take a drastic turn before you know it.

New Life After the Brokenness of Burnout

Freedom from the past opens new doors to regain vision, passion, and the desire to lead again.

The exciting element of working through burnout is the new life awaiting you. Some things in life can be born from something dead. Essentially, a caterpillar dies and is resurrected into a butterfly with the same juices that gave the creature its original form. A similar process brings a resurrected life from a fatigued, worn-out, and burned-out soul. I hope this is your story, and if it is not, it *can* be your story.

My dead caterpillar-like life was brought to a fresh and exciting life through a process of healing and time. I will not go into detail about planting a new church but rather provide a synopsis. A small group of individuals gradually gathered around me. We developed a church "startup team" for a portable church. This team consisted of around fifty people to set up, take down, teach, lead worship, and love people. A plan was developed to begin the church with two pre-services and launch in the third month. On our first pre-service, more than 180 people showed up. That was a fantastic beginning, but it was also the lowest attended service the church has ever had.

We began in a public school in Crowley, Texas, where the church met weekly for more than three years. After that, we moved to a shopping center and remodeled it to fit the church's needs. We are currently in the same location. Our church is the Fountains Fellowship Church, Crowley, Texas, and we also have a second church campus in Fort Worth, Texas. Both churches provide a complimentary café, nursery, and preschool, fifth-grade children's classes, a worship team, and live teaching. Our ministries touch thousands of people's lives in our area and globally through our foreign mission outreach in Romania, Ukraine,

Thailand, Myanmar, and Kenya. More than 50,000 different people have walked through the doors of our campuses.

We have been blessed with a group of sacrificing, amazing people who get the job done. We attempt to reach out to the community on both of our campuses to extend love, life, and hope to the hopeless. We have seen many lives changed for the better, and we continue to *"share our story."*

Keep growing and allow your brokenness and burnout to become the foundation of your dreams and vision of great plans in the package of your life. You can and you will do great things!

I want to thank you for coming alongside me on the journey of overcoming burnout. Keep your head up and be on the lookout for other leaders you and I can help in their recovery from burnout. Feel free to check out some of my other resources and, if I can do anything to assist you, kindly reach out to me. I am a certified mental health life coach and love coaching, guest speaking, telling my story, and encouraging others. Please pass my book along and send anyone you may encounter who needs help with burnout to my website: www.donwomble.com

This is not the end—it is the beginning!

If you enjoyed this book, please take a few moments to write a review by visiting your favorite online retailer. Thank you!

Acknowledgments

I will forever be indebted to my wife, Kathy, who has stood by my side when it would have been easier to do otherwise.

I want to thank our children, Don II, Matthew, and Anna, for supporting me to lead others despite sometimes paying the price of their dad being a leader.

My sincere gratitude goes to Ken Dunn and Nicholas Boothman for teaching me the best way to write a book that others will want to read.

This book was made better by the editorial genius of Debra L Hartmann and her editorial team. I can't give enough praise and thanks to her for being honest with me with her comments, suggestions, and re-writes.

Thank you, Heather Koenig, for always making me look better with my work because of your work behind the scenes.

I am eternally grateful to my God for giving me the greatest privilege and purpose in life to love and lead people.

ABOUT THE AUTHOR

Don Womble has served as the CEO of two midsize 501(c)(3) organizations. He resigned after a twenty-five-year tenure at the first organization due to clinical burnout. Following two years of mental and physical recovery, Don learned how to emerge from burnout with a passion for leading again and a desire to help other leaders work through their own burnout.

Don has earned several college degrees, including an MBA in Organizational Psychology Development. In 2017, he co-founded a professional counseling center in his community. Don has achieved certification with the John Maxwell Team as a speaker, teacher, and coach and possesses a certification as a Mental Health Life Coach. Don is the published author of several books and courses and currently serves on the board of directors for three charitable organizations.

From childhood through adult life, Don Womble lived with Generalized Anxiety and Panic attacks. He is familiar with the fear and battles of those who agonize over these struggles. Don has learned by trial and error how to work through these disorders. Through the techniques and tools he has attained, he has provided teaching, mentoring, and assistance to countless individuals suffering from the same challenges.

Don, his wife Kathy, and his family live in south Fort Worth, Texas. He considers himself a family man and enjoys family events more than any other activities.

Please visit **DonWomble.com** to sign up for our mailing list and receive helpful tips, promotions, upcoming events, and more!

Connect with Don Womble on Social Media:

Facebook: Don Womble

Instagram: DonWombleSr

Twitter: DonWombleSr

LinkedIn: Don Womble

BOOKS BY DON WOMBLE

Attack Anxiety (Winning the Fight)

Fear Revival (Scars of the Tormented)

Printed in the USA
CPSIA information can be obtained
at www.ICGtesting.com
LVHW030428260924
792118LV00008B/14